T0282117

...ᴀɪꜱᴇ ꜰOR

UNCOPYABLE YOU

Dive into the transformative wisdom of *Uncopyable You* by Kay and Steve Miller. Discover your unique qualities, create a battle plan, and leverage these insights to enhance yourself and your impact. This book is your guide to unlocking the power of your authentic, uncopyable self.

Mark Hess
Hess Industries Ltd

Steve and Kay Miller's latest book, *Uncopyable You,* offers an insightful and compelling perspective on the importance of personal branding. We're living in an era when everyone is vying for attention, both personally and professionally. Their quote, "Personal branding is differentiating yourself and making yourself impossible to forget—forever," encapsulates the essence of their message beautifully.

Kate Strachnyi
Founder of DATAcated

Uncopyable You is more than a book for me; it was wake-up call to level up my personal branding. For anyone feeling a bit lost in the whole personal branding maze, this book is your personal GPS. It goes beyond just making you look good—it's about digging deep, finding what's genuinely you, and owning it.

Jasmin Bonkowski
Master Your Mindset, Transform Your Life:
Hypnosis for Lasting Success & Balance

In *Uncopyable You,* Kay and Steve offer a clear plan of action and pose the right questions to help identify your niche in any industry. I wholeheartedly recommend this book as an invaluable guide to personal and professional success. It not only inspires but equips readers with the tools necessary to carve out their own path to success. *Uncopyable You* is a must-read for anyone aspiring to stand out in their field and shape a bright future.

Rick Brassfield
Owner, The Hair Lounge

Uncopyable You contains a secret compass to point you toward *your* success. It will help you release strengths within that make you and your personal brand compelling, needed, and *uncopyable.* Brands should be like fingerprints—not copies. Each brand should be unique. It's time to bring out what you've already felt about yourself. Read it and use it so you can share your *Uncopyable You* with the rest of us.

Joe Snyder
Freightliner Custom Chassis
Marketing & Training Manager

Kay and Steve Miller have created a blueprint for engaging our stakeholders in meaningful and memorable ways.

Mark T. Miles, Ph.D.
President & CEO
Orscheln Management Co.

Uncopyable You by Steve and Kay Miller is a must-read for anyone looking to build a standout personal brand, especially in today's AI-driven world. They offer practical strategies for using AI as a tool to enhance, not replace, human connection and authenticity.

Shama Hyder
CEO & Founder, Zen Media

UNCOPYABLE YOU

sound
wisdom.
Because Your Success Matters

Sound Wisdom Books by
Steve and Kay Miller

Uncopyable Sales Secrets: How to Create an
Unfair Advantage and Outsell Your Competition

Stealing Genius: The Seven Levels
of Adaptive Innovation

Uncopyable: How to Create an Unfair
Advantage Over Your Competition

UNCOPYABLE YOU

YOU

CREATE A
PERSONAL BRAND
THAT GETS PEOPLE TO
KNOW YOU, LIKE YOU,
TRUST YOU, AND
REMEMBER YOU!

STEVE & KAY MILLER

© Copyright 2024– Steve and Kay Miller

All rights reserved. This book is protected by the copyright laws of the United States of America. No part of this publication may be reproduced, stored in or introduced into a retrieval system, or transmitted, in any form or by any means (electronic, mechanical, photocopying, recording or otherwise), without the prior written permission of the publisher. For permissions requests, contact the publisher, addressed "Attention: Permissions Coordinator," at the address below.

Published and distributed by:

SOUND WISDOM
P.O. Box 310
Shippensburg, PA 17257-0310
717-530-2122

info@soundwisdom.com

www.soundwisdom.com

While efforts have been made to verify information contained in this publication, neither the author nor the publisher assumes any responsibility for errors, inaccuracies, or omissions. While this publication is chock-full of useful, practical information; it is not intended to be legal or accounting advice. All readers are advised to seek competent lawyers and accountants to follow laws and regulations that may apply to specific situations. The reader of this publication assumes responsibility for the use of the information. The author and publisher assume no responsibility or liability whatsoever on the behalf of the reader of this publication.

The scanning, uploading and distribution of this publication via the Internet or via any other means without the permission of the publisher is illegal and punishable by law. Please purchase only authorized editions and do not participate in or encourage piracy of copyrightable materials.

ISBN 13 TP: 978-1-64095-525-7

ISBN 13 eBook: 978-1-64095-526-4

For Worldwide Distribution, Printed in the U.S.A.

1 2024

From Kay

To Steve, my best friend, my partner in business and life. You're still the one!

To Kelly, my daughter, the light of my life, and my inspiration. I'll love you forever.

To YOU, the reader who is committed to being Uncopyable. You've got this!

From Steve

As always, to my girls!

CONTENTS

FOREWORD

"If I had a longer time, I would have
written you a shorter letter."

—Mark Twain

Brevity is the soul of wit, and in this book, Steve and Kay have, indeed, given the reader a "shorter letter" full of wit. In *Uncopyable You*, they have cracked the code and given each entrepreneur, and would-be entrepreneur, a lexicon to one of the most vexing and important facets of organizational development—the personal brand.

Entrepreneurship has been called many things, perhaps the definition I like the most is that state of "relentless pursuit of opportunity with means currently beyond your control." (Attributed to Prof. Howard Stevenson, Harvard Business School, emeritus.) But what the authors, here, are saying is that it is NOT your relentless pursuit, not your *entrepreneur-ness*, not even your amazing product or innovative service that makes you memorable and magical, it is your personal brand. That alone makes an *Uncopyable You*, and to be one of the greats, you cannot go without it.

From the moment I first met Steve, he had my best interest at heart. You know this type of person the moment you meet them. They connect. For years, I have wondered what it was that gave him that 3rd eye, that 3rd ear, the ability to listen and to see and to connect. Now, after reading his latest book, I know. Steve has a radar for authenticity and how to pull it out of your soul. He saw my potential for a personal brand, and he began to pull it out of me. He is persistent and patient, and unrelenting in his belief in this idea. In *Uncopyable You*, he shares his wisdom and gives each reader a window into his method.

Henry David Thoreau is quoted as saying *"Most men lead quiet lives of desperation, and go to the grave with the song still in them."* This transcendental philosophy is as cutting as it is true, but there is good news, this doesn't have to be you. Steve and Kay start at the beginning and build a road map for all types for how to recognize a personal brand and what thought experiments and efforts need to be made confidently to build your own.

Follow this at your own peril (it will change you) ... or don't ... at your own peril you will slink through your effort with a song inside. Steve does not promise it will be easy. It is, of course, work; but it will make you memorable, and in the end, even if the memory of you is one of being shy, quiet and retiring, his pledge is to dig out your very self and to emblazon it on people's memory.

Join the movement of 1—your authentic self—and let Steve and Kay be your guide to this expansion and growth.

John B. Rogers, Jr.
Co-Founder and CEO Haddy Life
"alive in all rooms"

1

THE BIG IDEA

Uncopyable personal branding
empowers you to create your own
rules of competition to attract the right
people toward you and your mission.

Let's play a word association game.

Quick: What do you think of when you see the name "Steve Jobs"?

Think of at least three words that name makes you think of. Sorry, "Apple," or "Pixar," or any Apple product *doesn't* count. We're looking for adjectives *about* him. Do this right now, please.

What words did you come up with?

We did this exercise ourselves. Kay came up with *disruptive, unconcerned with what others thought of him, built his own box, one-of-a-kind,* and *controversial.* Steve thought of *visionary, insanely great, demanding,* and *charismatic.*

Steve Jobs has a clear personal brand. And he is UNCOPYABLE.

Before we continue our Steve Jobs breakdown, we ask you another question: What words or phrases would people say about *you*, if asked? Do you know? Do you know yourself?

Those words are your personal brand.

Does that make you happy? Can you build a personal branding strategy around those words? Do these words make you UNCOPYABLE?

Hey, we're assuming you're reading our book because you recognize the importance of standing out in today's world.

More than a decade has gone by since Jobs passed away. Yet we would be willing to bet that, somehow, he remains a present-tense reality for you, and that the instant you read his name just now, you knew exactly who he is—not was, *is*. We would also be willing to bet you had a strong sense of what Steve Jobs stands for—not stood for, *stands* for.

In fact, you can probably picture Steve Jobs right now, in that distinctive black turtleneck he made famous each time he took the stage to unveil the latest Apple product. You may even recall some of his words from Apple's "Think Different" ad campaign. For instance:

> *Here's to the crazy ones. The misfits, the rebels, the trouble-makers, the round pegs in the square holes, the ones who see things differently. They're not fond of rules.... You can quote them, disagree with them, glorify or vilify them. About the only thing you can't do is ignore them. Because they change things—they push the human race forward. And while some may see them as the crazy ones, we see genius. Because the people who are crazy enough to think they can change the world, are the ones who do.*

Did any of that ring a bell?

Our question to you now is: *Why do you know all that?*

Why do so many people seem to know so much about Steve Jobs? Why do we remember him? Why does he still show up as a presence in our world, a standard in our thinking about what is possible, and an influencer of our plans and decisions? Why, long after his death in 2011, do we remember what Steve Jobs stands for? Why (to get to the heart of the matter) do we feel as if we have connected directly, and in a memorable way, not just with his products, but with his personality?

It's not just that Jobs invented and launched cool stuff. Think about it. The transistor is arguably a far cooler invention than the iPhone (well, at least to Steve's dad, an electrical engineer) since the iPhone (and hundreds of other modern inventions) would have been impossible without it. Yet John Bardeen, Walter Brattain, and William Shockley, the inventors of the transistor—which, by the way, has been called the most important technological breakthrough of the twentieth century—may not be names, personalities, and faces you are familiar with. They may not stand for anything in particular in your mind. Whereas Steve Jobs is. And does.

Face it. At some level, you feel like you know this guy. Why?

Let's play another word association game—one you may find easier to play if you're under the age of, say, 25. What do you think of when you read the words "Mr. Beast"? What words come to mind? Please do the same experiment, right now. By the way, if you happen to be older than 25, maybe ask this question of the teenager or young adult you know best.

The odds are good that, in response to this question, words similar or identical to the ones on the following list rose immediately to the surface: *generous, giving, unselfish, give away, game, gaming, stunt, challenge, funny, rich,* and *creative.*

Right?

If you don't happen to be in Mr. Beast's target demographic, he is a You-Tuber currently in his mid-twenties who pioneered a new and immensely popular genre of video, one based on giving large sums of money to worthy recipients. At this writing he has more than 210 million subscribers on his platform, and he is active in supporting environmental causes.

Just as with Steve Jobs, we are betting that (if you are younger than about 25) Mr. Beast is an established personality for you, someone you feel as though you know personally, even though, technically, you know you don't.

Again: Why?

Why do so many people seem to know precisely the same things about an unassuming 24-year-old from Greenville, North Carolina? Why do they know what he does, what he looks like, and what he stands for? Why do they feel they know him on a personal level?

Here are two more examples:

What words come to mind when you read the name "Mary Kay"?

What do you think of when you read the name "Mark Twain"?

For "Mary Kay," did words such as *passion, cosmetics, empowering women,* and *entrepreneurial spirit* come to your mind?

For "Mark Twain," did you think of descriptive words like *wit, humor, writer, white suit, outspoken, independent, Tom Sawyer, Huck Finn,* and *skeptical?*

Those are the responses we came up with. Maybe the words you came up with had some common themes with the ones we have just shared here.

Now for the big question: Of the four people we've mentioned in this chapter, how many would you say that you somehow have the feeling you know them—even though you've never met them? Or to put it another way, how many of these names and personalities were familiar to you before you started reading this book?

So what exactly is going on?

Here's our answer. All of these people knew how to build and reinforce a **personal brand**—a brand that left even total strangers with the powerful sense that they knew them *as individuals*. And each of them *fused* that brand with a mission or an organization that became an extension of themselves and set them apart, forever, from any possible competition. They did that so well that, in the case of Twain and Jobs, many people *still* feel they know these individuals years or even decades after they died—and *still* consider them utterly unique! Which, to be fair, they are.

For each of these individuals, the approach that created and sustained the most important professional breakthroughs was built around a single, endlessly influential, endlessly applicable *big idea*. A big idea is one that has inspired millions of people down through the years, including us—and one we invite you to be inspired by now.

PERSONAL BRANDING
IS DIFFERENTIATING
YOURSELF TO MAKE
YOURSELF IMPOSSIBLE
TO FORGET—FOREVER.

THE BIG IDEA

Creating a personal brand that prompts and encourages people to know you, like you, trust you, and **remember** you!

UNCOPYABLE personal branding empowers you to create your own rules of competition—not just get out of the box, but to build your own box, carving out a unique, memorable space for yourself in your world and a space that attracts the right people to you and your mission.

That's why we wrote this book to help you create your big idea—whether you are a solopreneur seeking to expand your impact, someone who is thinking about becoming a solopreneur, or someone currently working as a contributor to one or more teams. If your aim is not just to become more successful, but more *unparalleled*, we wrote this book for you.

Personal branding, as each of these remarkable cases demonstrate, is the key to making good things happen in your world.

And we're here to help you do just that.

Let's get started by looking a little more closely at how each of these personal branding superstars gave you the feeling that you somehow know them personally. That's the subject of our next chapter.

Be sure to get your free resources at Uncopyableyou.com/resources

2

BE VISIBLY AND MEANINGFULLY DIFFERENT

Meet five uncopyable rockstars who exemplify innovative personal branding as well as seven uncopyable branding tactics.

Steve Jobs. Mr. Beast. Mary Kay. Mark Twain. Each of these remarkable people became a true *uncopyable rockstar* in personal branding. Our question is: What made that possible?

It wasn't that they were born with the knowledge and experience they needed about how to create and support a unique, powerful personal brand. Nobody is born with that. The truth is, each one became rockstars because *they **took action** in specific areas where they knew action could make a difference.* They noticed what worked. And they learned as they went along.

At some point, each of them made a fateful choice—to *do something different,* something that set their message and their mission apart from everyone else's. And then, having moved beyond their comfort zone once, they noticed the outcome, adjusted as necessary—and then did something different again. In other words, they made standing out from the crowd an operating philosophy, as well as a strategic objective. This is a neglected art that you can revive and use to your advantage.

Make no mistake—this really is how each of those amazing individuals moved the needle away from anonymity and toward visibility, recognition, and the status of being *known in the field of their choice*, even by people they had never met. Each found a way to turn the philosophy of *doing something different* into a specific, actionable plan—a plan that took the Big Idea you saw in the previous chapter from abstract idea into tangible reality.

Right now, it's time for *you* to act. It's *your* turn to do something different, something that most people do *not* do—including all those people out there right now who are competing with you for eyeballs, engagement, and revenue.

So here's a three-part challenge specifically designed to set you apart from the pack. *Warning:*

You should only take on this challenge if you are truly serious about building and supporting your own uncopyable personal brand through action. Assuming that is the case, please do feel free to read on.

Your Challenge: Step One

First, pick your favorite person from the following list. For the purpose of this exercise, consider this person to be your personal role model. Important: You don't have to know everything there is to know about your "branding superhero." You just need to know who they are, admire

MAKE STANDING OUT FROM THE CROWD YOUR OPERATING PHILOSOPHY, AS WELL AS YOUR STRATEGIC OBJECTIVE.

what they stand for in the larger world, and feel good about what they inspire you to believe is possible in *your* world. Here's the list again:

Steve Jobs

Mr. Beast

Mary Kay

Mark Twain

Pick one of these people right now. (Note: You can pick a different person as your role model later on if you want, but for the purpose of this challenge, stick with the rockstar you choose from this list.)

Your Challenge: Step Two

Take another look at that Big Idea we shared with you in the previous chapter. We're repeating it because it's worth emphasizing and worth remembering. *Don't* try to memorize it. *Do* read it closely a few times. *Do* become familiar with it, familiar enough for you to feel good about returning to it whenever you choose to remind yourself why you're making a personal commitment to improve your own personal branding.

THE BIG IDEA

> The Big Idea means to create a personal brand that prompts and encourages people to know you, like you, trust you, and **remember** you!

UNCOPYABLE personal branding empowers you to create your own rules of competition—not just get out of the box, but to build your own box, carving out a unique, memorable space for yourself in your world and a space that attracts the right people to you and your mission.

Your Challenge: Step Three

Now, think of *something specific you know your branding hero did to fulfill this Big Idea, something that other people did not do.* This action you consider could take several forms, including:

- Distinctive Appearance and Presentation Style

- Philanthropy and Stunts

- Unique World View

- Engagement with Fans

- Empowerment of Women

- Distinctive Literary Voice

- A Personal Mission

Search the Internet for this challenge if you want. Take a few minutes to read about this person.

Look for a specific action your personal branding rockstar took that set that person apart in keeping with the Big Idea you just read.

Obviously, there are no wrong answers to this challenge. As long as you took even a little time to evaluate your personal branding rockstar and identify something they chose to *do different* from the rest of the pack, you got it right. And you can continue to get it right, because each of these individuals is a seemingly never-ending source of unco- pyable personal branding innovations. Each could be the subject of a book of this length.

Uncopyable Personal Branding Best Practices

We invite you now to compare your answers to our answers and preview some of the breakthrough *uncopyable personal branding best practices* they exemplify, practices that we explore in the chapters that follow. These are the habits, the consistent behaviors that make people stand out from the crowd, and make compelling, memorable personal branding possible.

Disclaimer: Each of these extraordinary people did *much more* than the single uncopyable branding practice we are about to mention. We're just choosing *one* personal branding best practice for each rockstar right now to give you a clear idea of how that branding practice can help *you make standing out from the crowd your operating philosophy, as well as your strategic objective.*

For us, **Steve Jobs** exemplifies the uncopyable branding practice of ***benchmarking outside your chosen industry***. Anybody can imitate their direct competitors. Successful personal branding means identifying great ideas from worlds that your competitors *haven't even thought of exploring*. You'll learn more about Jobs and this powerful, foundational branding practice in Chapter 4. You'll also meet other people who have used this powerful uncopyable branding practice to create a niche in the area of their choice.

For us, **Mr. Beast** is a perfect representative of the uncopyable branding practice of ***being true to your personal value set, your mission, and your personal and organizational rules***. Another, more concise, phrase for this is "being authentic." And those two words really do capture the essence of what we're talking about here. What do you stand for? (If you don't know, your target market won't know, either.) What are you committed to doing, delivering, and denting the universe with? (Ditto.) What do you value, personally and professionally? What, in short, is your mission? Why do you do what you do? What vision supports that mission? What principles and operational standards support that mission that you will never, ever compromise? You'll learn all about why this branding practice is so important to your personal brand in Chapter 5, where we will also share examples from our own business that illustrate, in a compelling way, the power of being genuine in support of your personal brand.

For us, the life and legacy of **Mary Kay Ash** is a testament to the enduring power of *creating anchors and triggers that uniquely evoke your personal brand*. Mary Kay made the color pink a personal branding message, as well as a branding message for her organization. That didn't happen by accident. It was part of a carefully crafted plan she designed to build strong positive associations by using time-tested principles of perception, psychology, and persuasion. In Chapter 6, you learn how she built and executed that plan, how we built an anchors-and-triggers plan to support our own business after having been inspired by her example, and how we helped others to create powerful anchors-and-triggers plans in support of *their* personal brand.

For us, **Mark Twain** is an enduring role model in the realm of *finding and leveraging the right platforms for broadcasting your personal branding message*. You may think of Twain first and foremost as a great writer, and he certainly was that, but it's important to understand that he was also a master in the art of getting his voice heard. Twain knew that connecting with people through the medium of their choice was what kept his personal brand alive. He used lots of varied strategies for what we would today call "engaging" with his audience—and most of those strategies took him far beyond the desk where he wrote out his manuscripts in longhand. You'll learn more about this essential uncopyable branding practice in Chapter 8. In that chapter, you also meet a modern-day master in platform messaging strategy.

There's someone else we haven't mentioned, **Malala Yousafzai**. To us, she embodies the uncopyable branding practice of *seizing opportunities from apparent setbacks*. Her personal story is a truly remarkable one. We believe it will empower you as you learn to identify value, potential, and branding inspiration in literally every obstacle you encounter—and as you practice and perfect the non-negotiable deliverable of getting your message across to your target audience in a way that resonates. You get a close-up on Malala's mastery of this practice in Chapter 9, and you also hear another story about adversity that we think is just as powerful.

By the way, another uncopyable branding practice is *knowing your unique strengths and playing to them*. This is a best practice that all five of these rockstars share in common. You'll find out more about that brand-transforming, life-transforming habit in Chapter 7, and also hear some personal examples of how we've focused on our own uncopyable strengths. And just as important, how we delegate areas where we're not so strong to other people, so we can focus our efforts on building and strengthening the brand.

How Did Your List Compare with Ours?

Looking back at your list for your rockstar, did you notice any overlaps? If your list seemed entirely different from ours, that's fine, too. What matters most is that you start noticing and picking up on the specific areas where you can make yourself uncopyable for your target audience—that special, clearly defined group we call your "Moose." (We explain that term in Chapter 3.)

The whole point of this challenge is to inspire you to start identifying the specific to-do items to help you *create a unique impact with your brand messaging and in your world*, so you can start acting in those areas consistently.

Because ultimately, that's what this book is all about—taking action. In Chapter 10, you pull together everything you've learned about personal branding. You'll *design and begin to execute your personal battle plan.* You also receive significant guidance from us on how to monitor your progress toward important goals. And there are times when you need to know how to figure out when it's time to change tactics in response to changing circumstances, without changing your vision or your values—we cover that too.

That's what we're here for. If what you just read is what *you're* here for, let's get to work.

Be sure to get your free resources at Uncopyableyou.com/resources

3

FIND YOUR MOOSE

Specifically target clients and customers
with the value you deliver.

It's time to get to work. If you've made it this far in the book, we're willing to bet that two or more of the following questions are relevant to your world. Your task now is a simple one: Identify the questions that *you* THINK are pertinent, then answer them honestly, either YES or NO.

Whether you're a solopreneur, small business owner, freelance contributor, or full-time member of a team:

1. Have I effectively differentiated myself in a saturated market?

In markets crowded with competitors, standing out is crucial. Understanding how to effectively differentiate yourself and your offerings can be a pressing concern.

2. Am I employing the right strategies to build and maintain a strong online presence?

In a digital age, having a robust online presence is crucial for networking, attracting clients, and building a reputable brand.

3. Am I able to measure the ROI (Return on Investment) of my personal branding efforts?

Assessing the effectiveness of personal branding strategies and their impact on business growth is essential for continual improvement.

4. Am I managing negative reviews or feedback online in a way that protects my reputation?

Online reputation management is a concern, and understanding how to handle negative feedback in a constructive manner is vital.

5. Am I effectively communicating my values and expertise to my target audience?

Clear communication of your values and expertise is crucial to attract the right clients and opportunities.

If any of those questions rang a bell for you, and if you gave at least one NO response, we're thinking there's a very good chance you are not yet hunting Moose. And that's where any successful personal branding journey needs to start—by mastering the art of hunting Moose.

(For the origin of this "Moose hunting" strategy, which is a story all its own, see Chapter 9 of this book. It features a detailed description of the "Moose breakthrough" that changed our lives. We owe that breakthrough to a fateful discussion with the late Reverend Robert H. Schuller.)

Moose Hunting

Hunting Moose is a core branding lesson of the *Uncopyable Philosophy*, a lesson we've carried with us and shared with our clients for decades. It is also a marketing lesson; but please understand before you can market effectively, you need to do some meaningful *examination* of the market, and some meaningful examination of yourself.

Full disclosure: That is what you are embarking on here, a close look at your market and yourself, and it may take some time and attention. Investing that time and attention is what we ask our clients to do. It's what you need to do now.

For our part, we've been practicing hunting our own Moose for more than 37 years, because that's the point at which Steve (Miller, not Jobs) determined that he was, in fact, unemployable, which meant it was time to find a way to earn a living on his own.

Whether that's your situation or not (and we believe you're in very good company if it is), we want to challenge you to consider the possibility that this chapter's topic—the overlooked skill of hunting Moose—must be the strategic foundation of *all* your personal branding efforts. Hunting Moose is how you create and maintain long-term relationships, and also how you define your brand message, maintain the right current relationships with your customers, and attract new, mutually beneficial relationships with both customers and allies.

So what exactly is hunting Moose? It's target marketing—done the right way. Hunting Moose is knowing, with granular precision, *exactly* what kind of people you deliver value to and can expect to be paid by so you can connect and interact more consistently and effectively with those people, and invest your precious time and attention in building relationships with them.

Here's why we call this first principle of branding "hunting Moose." Imagine for a moment the world is a forest. Like any other forest, it is full of different animals—bears, birds, rabbits, deer, wolves, moose, squirrels, you name it. Now you have made the conscious decision that your product or service is best suited for Moose. The Moose represents your target market. You're interested *only* in Moose, not any other animal.

Every successful personal branding strategy starts with defining and understanding your Moose, because only when you understand your target audience can you expect to make and fulfill a big brand promise that resonates with your ideal buyer and also makes business sense for you.

Not everyone is the same. We're all different, with different needs and interests. Hunting Moose means understanding the differences that define the people who will respond to and rely on your brand promise—the people who will benefit at a memorably high level when working with you or buying from you.

Hunting Moose means knowing *how* they benefit, knowing how to distinguish them from everybody else, and knowing what interests them most so you can prioritize your time and attention intelligently. And the hard reality, the reality we are challenging you to address

THE ESSENCE OF YOUR BRAND IS THE BIG, YET SPECIFIC PROMISE YOU MAKE TO YOUR IDEAL TARGETS—YOUR MOOSE. **TO KNOW WHAT PROMISE YOU CAN MAKE THAT RESONATES WITH YOUR TARGET AUDIENCE, YOU MUST KNOW WHAT KIND OF MOOSE YOU ARE HUNTING!**

directly in this chapter, is that if you answered NO to even one of the questions you read at the beginning of this chapter, there is an excellent chance you are, at the moment, one of the many, many people who struggle with Moose hunting. But fear not. We're here to help.

Most people we talk to about personal branding make the mistake of thinking *everyone* should want or need the product or service they offer. They try to appeal to the entire universe. Or they make a very similar mistake—they try to appeal to some segment of the universe that either *doesn't benefit* from their value at a memorably high level, or *won't pay appropriately* for that value. Either way, that's a problem. And you have to solve that problem before you can build a powerful personal brand.

Meet Kate Strachnyi, a data and AI professional who's built a stellar brand in a male-dominated industry in a short period of time. In 2020, Kate founded DATAcated, a media company. Since then, her business has exploded. In addition to her media work, she's built a community, written a book, and much more. Oh, and as of October 2023, she has 169,000 LinkedIn followers.

Kate's passion is data, a field she was drawn to after she felt she needed to make a change in her career. Since the switch, Kate has established herself as an expert by consistently posting content on LinkedIn that's valuable to her Moose. (She uses other platforms too, but LinkedIn has been the most effective by far.)

The important lesson here is Kate is laser-beam focused on the data industry. It's not glamorous, but she loves data! Best of all, it's more than big enough for Kate to have a highly successful career! She knows her Moose and takes very good care of them!

Kate is super smart, but she's also authentic and likable. Her personal brand combines both her professional and personal side. About

90 percent of her content is professional and 10 percent is personal. She keeps her family life private, but happily shares her hobbies, including her love of running, hiking, and her recent foray into playing the guitar. She uses a lot of visuals, and is great on video, something she admits she had to work at. Follow her, and you'll feel like she's a friend.

We've had the opportunity to get to know Kate personally, and she's exactly as she seems—a very sharp dynamo who has a sense of humor and likes to have fun. She's also someone who goes out of her way to lift up others. As we write this, she's raising money to fight pediatric cancer. She's also shared unsolicited endorsements of both our books with her many followers, something she didn't have to do, but means a lot to us!

Kate defines a personal brand as "What people say about you when you're not in the room." Well, she's not in the room, and that's what we say! (Follow Kate Strachnyi on LinkedIn: inkedin.com/in/kate-strachnyi-data/.)

Activity: Who Is Your Moose?

So who is your Moose? What kind of customers, specifically, are you hunting? And what big, specific promise do you make, or could you make, to such customers? Just as important: What kind of customers are you *not* hunting?

Take a moment now to identify your very best customer. Or if you don't have customers (or the right customers) yet, identify your ideal customer. This should be a relationship you would clone if you could somehow manage that, a relationship where everything clicks. This should be someone who gets significant value from you and is willing to pay, without hesitation or haggling, the price you both know is fair for that value. Enter or re-enter that relationship right now, in your mind. If the relationship doesn't exist yet, do a little research, and build a real-world scenario where you deliver, and are compensated fairly for, delivering this distinctive value. Whatever you do, be sure you experience or re-experience that relationship on an *emotional* level, and make sure the relationship inspires and energizes you. If it doesn't, find or imagine another customer! Got it?

Once you have done that, capture the specifics. You will need this information as we move forward together in this book.

In a separate document, we want you to jot down the *real-world value you delivered to that customer* and *the big, specific promises you kept.* Take some time with this. Give it some thought. It's worth getting right. As you consider this puzzle, bear in mind the wise words of Grateful Dead front man and branding guru, Jerry Garcia—who once observed: *"You do not merely want to be considered just the best of the best. You want to be considered the only ones who do what you do."*

When you've completed the initial activity, we want you to repeat the process, but in reverse. Re-enter the relationship you have, or had, with a *customer who is the polar opposite of ideal.* Spend less time on this part, but do complete it. It's important to know what you *don't* want to relive, or can't afford to relive. So briefly jot down, in that same document, a few sentences about the kind of customer you know for sure that you *do not* want to spend your time, attention, and energy on from this point forward. Give a couple of clear reasons *why* you don't want to invest in this kind of relationship anymore. (For instance: Investing time and attention in this relationship delivers subpar revenue, consumes very high amounts of critical resources, and never seems to result in referrals or higher-paying assignments.)

YOU CAN'T BUILD A POWERFUL PERSONAL BRAND IF YOU DON'T KNOW WHO YOU'RE BUILDING IT FOR— YOUR MOOSE!

The first customer you wrote about was your Moose. The second customer you wrote about was something else: a squirrel, maybe, or a rabbit. Who knows. The point is, once you know your Moose, everything else falls into place. Focus on your Moose!

Knowing your Moose is Step One. It's the beginning of the personal branding process. It's non-negotiable. If you put in the time and effort necessary to identify your Moose and understand your Moose's habitat, you will *instantly* get deeper clarity on what your brand promise should be. If you don't, you will copy (with underwhelming or even disastrous results) the brand promises of others, you will not deliver memorable value, and you will not stand out. *Effective personal branding is all about standing out by keeping a brand promise that is uniquely relevant to **your** Moose—not someone else's.*

So stop trying to shoot all the animals in the forest! Stop imagining that the fact that someone is willing to buy from you, or consider buying from you, makes them your Moose! It doesn't!

Instead, start noticing where the Moose are congregating! Start focusing on the issues that preoccupy your Moose! Start thinking about what constitutes "Moose bait" in your world! *Start hunting Moose—and only Moose!*

You must understand how your Moose defines the word "value" *in their world.* That may take a little research, which is fine. Remember, you can always go back to that document you created in the activity we shared with you earlier in this chapter and add to it or refine it. The critical imperative is to get the latest, best, and most accurate information about the challenges your Moose faces, the pain that challenge creates, and the degree to which you can promise to make that pain go away *and keep your promise.* When the potential to deliver value is clear, two decisions become very easy: 1) Your

TO THE DEGREE THAT
YOU UNDERSTAND
YOUR MOOSE BETTER
THAN ANYONE ELSE,
YOU WIN.

decision to engage with your Moose; and 2) their decision to listen to and trust your brand promise.

A Real-World Example

So far we've been talking in abstract terms. It's time to look at a specific, real-world example of *precision* Moose hunting.

Meet Katie "RV" O'Neill, one of our favorite representations of uncopyable personal branding. Recently Kay was hired to deliver a sales presentation to a major RV manufacturer. When she asked our client for a list of people to interview in preparation for the program, the client put Katie at the top of the list. As one of the top high-end RV salespeople in the nation, Katie is walking, talking, passionate proof that you don't have to be able to launch a viral global trend to use social media platforms in a persuasive, compelling, and memorable way that supports and extends your personal brand *by getting you right up close to your Moose.*

And by the way, if anyone tells you that the central element of your personal strategy for hunting Moose should be "invest in creating a video that receives tens of millions of views," turn and run away as fast as you can! Viral videos are, for most of us, impossible to predict ahead of time, which means that, for most of the people reading this book, this is not a realistic expectation. The idea is not to flood the whole world with your message—that's the polar *opposite* of hunting for Moose. The idea is to put something out there that *shows up* where you *know your Moose hang out*, something that is likely to *attract Moose.* And in that critical discipline, Katie "RV" O'Neill stands out as a true ninja warrior. (Follow Katie "RV" O'Neill on LinkedIn: https://www .linkedin.com/in/katie-o-neill-31a46810/.)

YOUR PROSPECTS AND CUSTOMERS ARE BUSY—LIKE YOU, THEY HAVE A LOT GOING ON. STAYING ON THEIR MIND IS KEY.

—KAY MILLER

Search on YouTube for "Katie RV O'Neill," or @rvsinsideout, and you'll come across a playlist that stands as one of our favorite examples of well-designed Moose bait: Scores of personal walk-throughs of jaw-dropping top-of-the line RVs available from Katie's employer, Transwest Truck Trailer RV of Frederick, Colorado. These are not just recreational vehicles, they're mobile luxury residences for people who expect to travel the great outdoors in high style! And that, for the record, is Katie's Moose—elite upscale consumers who love traveling, love the great outdoors, and have set luxury leisure and vacation experiences as a lifestyle priority.

Katie's Moose, her target audience, certainly isn't "everyone on earth," nor is it "everyone watching YouTube" or "everyone in the market for a recreational vehicle." These vehicles each typically cost a quarter of a million dollars *and up*, and Katie is very clear on the price ranges she's dealing with in each of her high-energy, high-style walkthroughs. There's a reason she mentions that, of course. She wants people who aren't Moose to tune out—and she wants people who *are* Moose to keep watching.

She knows exactly who she is talking to in her videos—high-net-worth individuals with a love for adventure and wilderness experiences and an equally intense love of five-star accommodations. Who says you can't have both when you want to make a road trip? Certainly not Katie! Listen in on one of her upbeat walkthroughs:

> *This model has an extremely large rear shower. I wanted to show you this wonderful rain head shower; you'll notice with our cathedral ceilings, we've got plenty of head room for someone who's really tall. Now, I am not really tall, but I would have lots of room if I were! We also have the removable shower head here, which is also adjustable, so you can*

slide this up and down. So, great controls. Also here in the back we've got shampoo, conditioner, and body wash dispensers built in. This is a really nice feature. For anybody who's traveled in an RV before, you know how hard it is to keep things from flying off the counter! The other thing that's really nice about this coach is that not only is it a full tile finish but it also has a great seat in the shower, so there's lots of room to shave your legs or wash your feet or whatever it may be that you need to do at the end of the day. And this horizontal detailing in the shower is pretty darn fancy; it's one of my favorite adornments, it matches my personality. Nice and sparkly! ...Okay, we're going to open the closet door and I have to tell you, this closet smells absolutely delicious. This is a cedar-lined closet with a ton of wardrobe space. You'll notice there's two bars here in front for shirts, so you can have a place to store shorter clothes, a little more extra storage. Lots of room!

Let's pause here and ask: Is Katie trying to hunt all the animals in the forest?

Of course not! She's hunting Moose. There's a very clearly defined group of potential customers she's talking to in these videos: Adventurers, travelers, and outdoors enthusiasts who can afford a three-quarter-of-a-million-dollar leisure vehicle. Everyone else can click onto a different video. But the people who *do* watch the whole walk-through, they're the people Katie wants to talk to, and vice versa.

Now, if you've been following along with all the concepts we've shared with you in this chapter, you know that Katie's not just supposed to identify the Moose she wants to hunt, she's also supposed to deliver on a big, specific *brand promise* she's making to those customers and potential customers.

Every time you communicate effectively with your target audience, you are setting out Moose bait. And every piece of Moose bait you set out must *implicitly or explicitly* lay out and reinforce your brand promise.

The following is a recent interview Kay did with Katie. Check out her answer to the very first question and notice the material we have put in *italics*.

Q. How would you describe your personal brand promise?

A. *I want every prospective client I meet to have a better life than they had before they met me.* I'm going to make sure that every single person I meet is better off having met me than they would have been not having met me. And if I do that, I know my life is going to improve. And I cannot tell you how true that is. Like if you stop worrying about you, and start worrying about how to serve other people, not just your clients, but also your employers, everything will come together behind it, and you don't have to worry about anything. And let me tell you how I got there. *I was first drawn to the automotive industry after a bad experience while attempting to purchase a vehicle for myself. Now my mission is making sure that never, ever happens to someone who is in the market for an RV. I am there to take care of them and help them make the absolute best decision they possibly can. That's what I am all about.*

Q. Even if that means they decide not to buy from you, right?

A. Correct. Sometimes they shouldn't buy. Sometimes they shouldn't move forward with a purchase. Sometimes my job is to inform someone about what I think the best move for them is, and it's not buying a vehicle. Sometimes my job is to say, "You know what, I know you came in to buy a B class van, because you want to live in it.

But it's really not such a good idea. And if you need to save up a little bit more so that you can move into this next level, this is what I would recommend." And here's the beautiful thing that happens when you do that: You keep them. More often than not, they turn into clients! They come back to you. They want to work with you. They tell their friends about you. Because these are big transactions, and they know you're a person of integrity, and they want to get it right.

Q. Which means keeping your brand promise?

A. Which means keeping my brand promise. Right.

Q. How do you know when you're talking to someone who's your Moose?

A. Personally, I'm a big believer in just asking questions. The more questions I ask, without any kind of preconceived notions, the more information I have about who I'm dealing with, and the clearer the picture is. So the first thing I would recommend to anybody about confirming whether or not someone is in the target market is to make it your goal to discover who it is you're dealing with, without any assumptions at all. In my world, that means asking questions like: How did you decide this vehicle is what you want to look at? What kind of research led you here? What do you have currently? What do you like about it? What don't you like about it? How are you going to use this vehicle? Oh, camping, got it, so how many people are typically going to be with you on these camping trips? How long do you plan on being out? Where do you like to go? How often do you see yourself using the vehicle? Make it about them. At the end of the day, when you make it about the other person, you are going to get so much insight. And you're going to stand out from the competition. You're going to have a real conversation. Whereas everyone else is just going to be saying "Let me show you what I have."

Magic Doesn't Happen Without the Moose

In future chapters, we return often to this concept of hunting the Moose, because as you now know, it's central to the development of your personal brand, and specifically, to the development of your personal brand promise. Once you know who the Moose is, you can figure out what the right brand promise is. Not before! Once you know what the right brand promise is, you can start making it and keeping it. Not before!

So, invest some time on this before you move on to the next chapter. Do a little more research. Ask a few more questions. Get a bit more clarity on who is, and isn't, the Moose you're going to be hunting. And if that promise energizes you, motivates you, excites you, inspires you—as Katie's brand promise so clearly inspires her—then the magic starts to happen. You start creating better and better Moose bait. And you start expressing your brand in more and more powerful, compelling, and impossible-to-forget ways.

By the way, did you notice that in talking about her brand, Katie started to tell a *story* about *why* she does what she does? Look at it again:

> *I was first drawn to the automotive industry after a bad experience while attempting to purchase a vehicle for myself. Now my mission is making sure that never, ever happens to someone who is in the market for an RV. I am there to take care of them and help them make the absolute best decision they possibly can. That's what I am all about.*

That's an essential expression of the personal brand known as *myth*. When we use the word "myth," we don't mean myth in the sense of something that isn't true. We mean it in the far older, far more important sense of a "narrative or story that confirms an important truth, and is repeated often."

You learn more in Chapter 5 about the art of turning your personal brand promise into a narrative, a powerful and unique story that is repeated over and over again—not just by you, but by employees, allies, and customers. For now, though, just focus on clarifying your Moose and your brand promise.

Three Important Questions and Answers

Stop, think, and then answer the following three most important questions:

1. *My Moose is...*

2. *The value I deliver to my Moose is...*

3. *My personal brand promise is...*

Be sure to get your free resources at
Uncopyableyou.com/resources

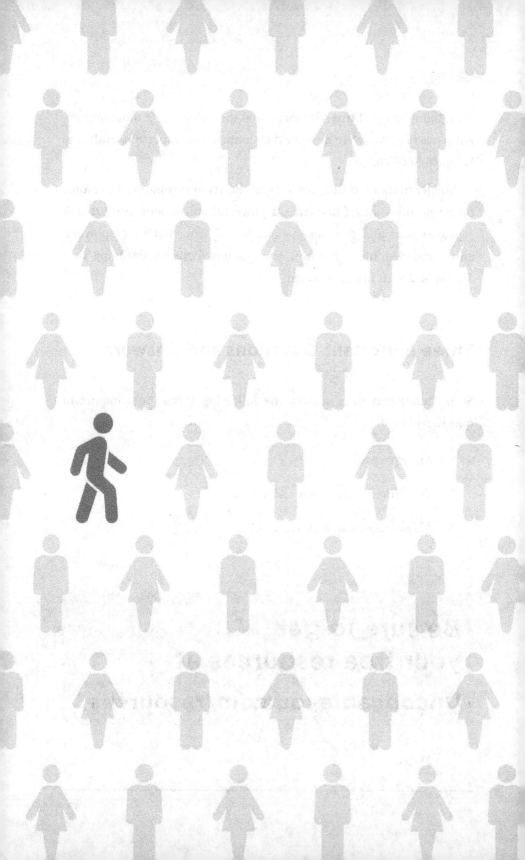

4

STEALING GENIUS FOR YOUR PERSONAL BRAND

Identify great ideas from worlds that your competitors haven't even thought of exploring.

Being uncopyable, in personal branding or in anything else, requires *innovating.* Yet innovation has long been, and remains, a much-misunderstood concept.

Many people we talk to think innovation is them sitting in a conference room, or logging on to a Zoom call, so they can keep tabs on what the competition is doing—so they can attempt to outdo X, whatever X is. Make no mistake—innovation is far more demanding and difficult than that. It takes commitment. It takes patience. It challenges you to look in places you may not be used to looking, and to think in ways you haven't been thinking up to now. Most people aren't willing to invest the time and energy necessary to truly innovate. That's because most people don't know what innovation is.

By the time you get done with this chapter, though, you won't be like most people.

Picasso and the Copier-Heads

Steve Jobs, one of our personal branding superheroes, left behind a personal and organizational legacy for all of us, a legacy that is synonymous with innovation. For most of the people we talk to about this, Jobs shows up at or near the top of the list of people who managed to make innovation a way of life. That commitment showed up consistently in his own life, in his organization, and in the marketplace. If you doubt that, stop to think of how many of his innovations *still* shape your life and the lives of others.

But there's a big question to consider. What *made* Jobs an innovator? What did he actually *do* to make himself and his company memorable in that regard?

Here's our answer: He *stole genius* from places where his competitors were unlikely to go looking for it. Steve Jobs was a master at keeping an eye out for great, high-impact ideas that might be relevant *to* his industry, but that originated *outside* his industry.

He knew those kinds of ideas were far less likely to be something his competition had in development. And he didn't want to just be better than his competition. He wanted to operate in a whole different universe than the competition did. So once he looked beyond the playground where his competition was playing, and he came across the right idea, guess what he did? He stole it. Notice that he didn't borrow the idea. Meaning he didn't take it on tentatively, or inauthentically, or without personalizing it. He *stole* it. He made the idea all his own by putting it in an entirely new context. This is the essence of innovation. This is what you have to do if you want to be uncopyable.

Perhaps the most famous example of Jobs stealing genius comes from the Apple product he launched that arguably did the most to turn the computer industry and society as a whole upside down—the Macintosh, the first truly user-friendly personal computer.

Everything about this machine, released back in 1984, was a game changer: its newfangled "mouse" (that most people still thought described a small, furry, bewhiskered animal), its image-driven, rather than text-driven, user interface (which eventually inspired Microsoft to develop the Windows operating system), and its quiet insistence that the document, rather than the application, was the foundation of the user experience. All of this seemed brand-new in 1985.

But was it?

In fact, every one of these breakthroughs originated at a copier company: Xerox.

Jobs's competitors weren't particularly interested in what a copier company had to say about computer design. Steve Jobs, on the other hand, was willing, able, and eager to do a little digging to figure out what interesting things people outside his industry were doing, so he could decide for himself whether their ideas could impact *his* industry: computers. And by doing that kind of digging, by stealing genius from an outside source, he found a way to leave, as he put it, a ding in the universe.

Later, Jobs would say of the breakthrough Macintosh design:

> *Picasso had a saying—"good artists copy, great artists steal"—and we have always been shameless about stealing*

great ideas. ...They [Xerox management] were copier-heads
who had no clue about what a computer could do...Xerox
could have owned the entire computer industry.[1]

Those words from Jobs make the case persuasively. He looked out-side his sandbox for the best ideas, then brought them back to the sandbox. We believe the concept of *stealing genius* really is essential to any deep understanding of Jobs, or for that matter, of any of the other personal branding rockstars we're introducing to you. *They all do this.*

Jobs was a master at it, of course, but every story we are sharing with you in this book was made possible by a clear grasp of the real-ity of innovation. It's looking outside your sandbox, finding something cool, and then memorably setting yourself apart from everyone else in the sandbox by bringing that cool thing back and defining yourself with it.

Do what Jobs did. Take on the role of Picasso. If you are serious about becoming uncopyable, look beyond what the people you com-pete with, or want to compete with, are doing. Then you can focus on a what people in other realms, other completely unrelated industries, other fields of specialization, other universes, are doing. Look long enough and passionately enough, and you will find something special you can make all your own by bringing it into the world you are creat-ing—the world of serving your Moose.

The Ad Without a Product

The key thing to understand about this idea of stealing genius is that it's *not* limited to technical disciplines like computer design. In fact, one of the most important examples of Jobs's looking outside of his own industry for inspiration connects to the masterful personal and corporate branding strategy he mapped out in the late 1990s. He stole its core concept from someone else, and not from a competitor in his industry. He stole it from a shoe company.

In a landmark 1997 speech at an employee town hall, Jobs said:

> *Nike sells a commodity, they sell shoes. And yet when you think of Nike, you feel something different than a shoe company. In their ads, as you know, they don't ever talk about the product, they don't ever talk about their air soles, how they're better than Reebok's air soles. What's Nike do in their advertising? They honor great athletes and they honor great athletics. That is what they are about.*

Now think back to that famous Apple TV ad we shared with you in Chapter 1. The script for that ad follows. Jobs himself narrated the commercial, which ran later in 1997, the same year he gave that speech to his employees. It is, in fact, the execution of the idea he shared with Apple employees during that town hall.

> *Here's to the crazy ones. The misfits, the rebels, the trouble-makers, the round pegs in the square holes, the ones who see things differently. They're not fond of rules.... You can quote them, disagree with them, glorify or vilify them. About the only thing you can't do is ignore them. Because they change things—they push the human race forward. And while some may see them as the crazy ones, we see genius. Because the*

people who are crazy enough to think they can change the world, are the ones who do.

As those powerful words resonated through millions of television screens, millions of people saw film clips of specific misfits, rebels, and troublemakers—people who, like Steve Jobs, were crazy enough to take a stand, *think* differently, and thereby *make* a difference. They didn't see any Apple products! What they saw instead were *people who changed the world by challenging its norms.*

They saw Albert Einstein smoking a pipe. They saw Bob Dylan preparing to step onstage. They saw Martin Luther King Jr. delivering his "I have a dream" speech. They saw Richard Branson descending from a zipline onto a huge Virgin logo and uncorking a bottle of champagne. They saw John Lennon and Yoko Ono singing during their bed-in for peace. They saw Buckminster Fuller demonstrating his geodesic dome. They saw Thomas Edison staring off into the distance in search of the next breakthrough inspiration. They saw Muhammad Ali shadow boxing and clowning for reporters. They saw Ted Turner beaming at a press conference and raising a victorious clenched fist. They saw Maria Callas, Mahatma Gandhi, Amelia Earhart, Alfred Hitchcock, Martha Graham, Jim Henson, Frank Lloyd Wright, and Pablo Picasso, each a visionary, each unique, each subverting the status quo in their own distinctive way.

And what those millions of TV viewers also saw as they watched that amazing 60-second ad, though hardly any of them realized it at the time, was Steve Jobs stealing genius from Nike.

Stealing Genius in Action

A fascinating little side note is in order here. Steve Miller, this book's co-author, knows for certain that this particular Steve Jobs principle— the principle of making breakthroughs by adapting ideas and best practices from outside your chosen field—wasn't just something Jobs did. It was, and no doubt still is, part of the Apple organizational culture. It was something he may have helped inculcate throughout the management team, something he spread outward through the entire employee base. How do we know this? Because we saw it in action firsthand.

Back in the early 1980s, probably 1982 or 1983, Steve (Miller) was exhibiting at a trade show in New York City. He was working with his brother at the time, and the event they were taking part in was known as a premium incentive show. The idea was that executives from all types of companies would show up, wander the aisles, and come across products that could be used as giveaways or incentives to reward employees for performance, for loyalty, or for hitting a career milestone, such as a five-year anniversary.

There were a variety of products for this trade show: Big, small, cheap, expensive, you name it, they ran the gamut. Steve and his brother, Scott, were having a good show. They had set up a good booth design. They offered custom engraving services on their products, which a lot of people were interested in. They had a good plan—aggressive preshow communications and a lot of experience when it came to attracting and interacting with prospective customers. As a result, there were a lot of high-quality conversations at their little booth.

Across the aisle, though, was a company with a far larger booth display. But while that booth had high traffic, it wasn't generating business, like Steve's. The booth's occupant: Apple Computer, Inc. (That's what it was called back then, by the way. This was not only before the release of the Macintosh, but also long before the company removed the word "computer" from its name.)

On the last day of the show, one of the guys from Apple walks over to Steve's booth. The Apple guy introduces himself. Steve remembers that the man's nametag read "Sales Director, Apple Computers." Steve has forgotten the man's name since that was the only time they interacted. Hey, it was forty years ago. But he knows for sure that he was dealing with the special markets Sales Director. Let's just call him Apple Guy.

Apple Guy asks, "Are you in charge of this booth?"

Steve nods and says, "Yep."

"Well, my name is Apple Guy (or whatever it was), and I'm the Special Markets Sales Director for Apple Computer, and you guys are kicking our ass. I'm here to find out how you're doing it. So, how are you doing it?"

That was a fateful question. It launched Steve's moonlighting consulting business! Apple Guy liked what Steve had to say in the conversation that followed. He connected Steve with a trade show marketing person in Palo Alto, California. Now we're not saying Steve Miller had any huge impact on Apple's strategic thinking. He never did get to meet Steve Jobs. But we are here to confirm that Steve Miller did share everything he knew about creating effective marketing plans for an organization attending a trade show, and that his words made a difference. Apple teams implemented, and appreciated, what was shared over the course of those few days in Palo Alto.

The real point of the story: *Steve became part of Apple's innovation process!* The principle at the heart of that process is just as relevant to you right now as it was to Apple back then:

*Don't just benchmark what your competitors are doing to get great results. Find out what people **outside your field of expertise** are doing to get a result that makes it easier for you to deliver value to your Moose so you can benchmark that!*

Before we go any further, we should give you a little background on that important word "benchmark."

The Deming Factor: Benchmarking

Because of Steve's father, as a teenager, Steve had the opportunity to spend a little time with W. Edwards Deming, one of the most important and impactful management consultants in the history of business. Deming's work is widely credited as one of the major factors in Japan's extraordinary economic growth in the decade following 1950. By the end of that decade, Japan was on a growth path that would eventually result in the country's economy ranking second in the world, second only to the United States. That rapid pace growth becomes astonishing when you realize that Japan was decimated on all fronts—economically, in terms of its infrastructure, and in terms of its standing in the world—at the end of World War II. That seemingly miraculous recovery was based directly on principles Deming developed to support his theory of Total Quality Management. One of the most important of those principles was the idea of benchmarking.

The definition of benchmarking that Steve was taught goes as follows: "To observe correct behavior and implement within your own context." But here's the point Deming shared with Steve (and anyone else who would listen): Observing correct behavior within your own industry, or your own field of expertise, only gives you a comparison.

It tells you how you're doing when you examine what's already known, what's already familiar.[2] In other words, *it's not innovation.*

If you really want to innovate, if you really expect to be uncopyable, you must do what Jobs did. You must move beyond your comfort zone and expose yourself to what we call *alien experiences.* Observing alien behavior that works often stimulates entirely new ways of looking at your world—and the best new ways to engage with and deliver value to the Moose you identified in Chapter 3!

The Adventurer Academic

One of our favorite examples of someone who has successfully leveraged alien behavior is our dear friend and former client Jessica Kizorek, the Badass Businesswoman.

A visionary entrepreneur, an international activist, a futurist, and a legendary video marketing pioneer, Jessica is best described as a force of nature. Since 2001, she has specialized in finding new personal and organizational mountains to climb, reaching the peak for each, and then raising her binoculars to her eyes to spot and target the next mountain on her itinerary. Every new journey has cannily leveraged insights, experiences, and out-of-the-box ideas from her past journeys—narratives and perspectives that instantly set her apart, even in the most crowded fields. She reminds us a bit of David Bowie, in the sense that her constant reinventions of herself always seem to draw on something consistent—a sense of adventure. Her next journey is always unique, always exciting, and always rooted in some striking and unexpected discovery that has gone before. The result? Like Bowie, Jessica is utterly impossible for any competitor to imitate! She's simply a category unto herself.

It all started with video production. Working primarily with large nonprofits through her company Two Parrot Productions (co-founded with her father Bill Kizorek), she created hundreds of short films and successful video-centric fundraising campaigns for clients such as the AARP Foundation, Special Olympics, and the Lions Club. She has now traveled to more than 60 countries, and has covered many humanitarian causes as both a journalist and documentarian.

At last count, Jessica has written eight books, many of which focus on marketing with video on the Internet. She is also the creator of *Make Them BEG*, a digital video educational product line designed to teach female entrepreneurs how to create an irresistible personal brand. The course won first place in the *Miami Herald's* Business Plan Challenge.

She also launched the BadassBusinesswomen.org project, which as of this writing has been supporting female entrepreneurs and executives for more than thirteen years. With the goal of providing both professional training and opportunities for meaningful relationship building, Badass Businesswomen creates incubator events, conferences, parties, and rich-media content for its target audience, and features this powerful insight on its website:

> *Unfortunately, a businesswoman who is strong-willed, ambitious and clear about her goals is too often labeled a "bitch." Being an edgy and vocal woman is not always celebrated in the business environment. Being a card-carrying Badass Businesswoman does not merely announce and unleash your inner badass. Consider us a tribe, coming together, challenging and mentoring one another in today's male-oriented business world.*

Now tell the truth. Is "announcing and unleashing your inner badass" the voice you would imagine hearing and the messaging you would expect to encounter from a professor delivering a college lecture? Probably not. Which brings us to Jessica's latest mountain—her latest leveraging of an alien experience into a sandbox that wasn't even remotely expecting it. She's soon going to be Jessica Kizorek, PhD.

It's true. Badass entrepreneur Jessica Kizorek, Magna Cum Laude, Phi Beta Kappa, graduate of University of Colorado Boulder with a degree in International Business, and a Master's degree in Global Strategic Communications from Florida International University. She is now closing in on earning her PhD in 2025 in Business Administration. By extension, she is closing in on the world of academia. The next Moose she's planning on hunting will be found on college campuses. She's more than ready to hunt in that world, but it's an open question whether it is entirely ready for her!

That's a good thing, of course. When it comes to stealing genius, you *want* to challenge people, challenge their preconceptions, broaden their horizons, and get them to consider new possibilities and new paradigms.

In a way, challenging people to set aside certainties, move beyond their comfort zone, and embrace possibility is the biggest mountain of all—the mountain Jessica has been scaling her entire life. Oh, did we mention she's also been a diplomat. An elite athlete. A conceptual artist who has created, among other things, an intricate electric LED installation rooted in the latest brain science, an installation written up in a positive review in *Psychology Today*.

Like we said. An adventurer.

Steve set up a Zoom interview with Jessica. The following are some highlights.

Q: So talk to me about the Doctorate. Not a lot of people who are as successful as you are make that career choice. What was your thinking?

A: I turned forty-two years ago, and I decided to go back and start my Master's; now I'm a year into my doctorate. I always said that if I didn't care about money, I would have been a college professor, and I just got to thinking about that. I make so much more money than a college professor does that now I'm in a position to be able to be both a college professor and take on professional projects at the same time. I mean, I can have both. So I'm really serious about transitioning into academia. Right now, I'm being recruited for a position at Florida International University where I did my Master's and where I'm working on my Doctorate. It's all looking good. I'm being recruited for a faculty position to basically run their multimedia department at the whole university. I'm very excited.

Q: How does your personal brand connect to all of this?

A: I'm definitely using my personal brand, the adventurer persona, and specifically the Badass Businesswoman, to help me make this transition. The adventurer has a way of opening people's eyes. The eagerness to compete without apology opens people's eyes. Outspokenness, for me, definitely has an impact. People are curious about what kind of classroom experience that's going to be. And at the same time, I'm relying on that personal brand more than ever to close deals and position myself for the next round.

Q: You describe yourself as an adventurer. Is that at the heart of your personal brand? And where does that come from?

A: Yeah. Adventure and competition. Those are two sides of the same coin, really. Call it "competitive adventure." But yes, everything, all the branding draws on that. I don't know if you know this about me, but I played tennis as a junior, I was ranked like second in the city of

Chicago as a teenager. It was no joke, I was a competitive player, and then I wrecked my shoulder. And so I found out that I was going to have to get surgery to fix my shoulder and I was going to have to sit out my freshman year. So I went to school, and I did not play tennis in school. Luckily, my parents had the resources to pay for my college. And then a bit later I got back into athletics, I started cycling in college. I got into track cycling. I was in Colorado and I trained at the Olympic Training Center in Colorado Springs. And at one point I was ranked second in the United States for the 500 meter track cycling event. So the athletic background is kind of the starting point. That's where the whole competitive adventure theme started out. And it came very naturally to me. It still does, because I am all about moving forward. I would never be able to just retire and, like, sit around all day. I would self-destruct. In fact, that's one of the big reasons I want to be in academia, because you can teach into your seventies and your eighties if you want to.

Q: You're like the Energizer Bunny out there. Just always doing something, always going places, always a badass. You're just so much fun to watch. What keeps you going?

A: Lots of things. One of them is knowing for certain you have a positive impact on people. When you see evidence of that, it makes all the hard work feel like it was no problem at all. That's a big reason I'm transitioning into academia, because you can get that direct evidence that you've helped someone. That's what I've loved about being a guest lecturer. You're face to face. But you don't have to be face to face. You know, as an email marketer, you send out these emails, and you have no idea who's reading them or what they think of them, whether they have any feelings about them. Then you'll get a message that says, " Oh, my God, I've been on your email list for 13 years. Thank you." That's great when that happens. (Follow Jessica Kizorek at jessicakizorek.com)

Steal Some Genius[3]

It's time to put this chapter's core idea into practice. It's time to move beyond your comfort zone and expose yourself to some *alien experiences*—and steal some genius!

Five action steps to consider:

1. Seek Inspiration Outside Your Field

Look for innovative ideas and practices in industries or fields different from your own. Explore how these ideas can be adapted to your specific circumstances or industry. For instance, if you're in tech, you might explore advancements in design or marketing strategies from the fashion or automotive industries.

2. Adopt a Mindset of Continuous Learning

Embrace a culture of continuous learning and curiosity. Keep abreast of new developments, technologies, and trends not only in your field but in other areas that might provide a fresh perspective or unexpected solutions to challenges you're facing.

3. Benchmark Against Uncommon Metrics

Instead of just benchmarking your strategies against competitors within your industry, look to successful strategies employed in other fields. Evaluate how those strategies achieve their results and consider how similar tactics could be employed in your own endeavors.

4. Engage with Diverse Communities

Engage with communities, forums, or networks outside your typical circles. Participate in discussions, attend events, or collaborate on projects that expose you to different ideas, perspectives, and experiences. This will not only broaden your horizon but could also spark innovative ideas that you could apply in your own field.

5. Experiment and Take Risks

Inspired by the adventurous spirit highlighted in the excerpt, consider stepping out of your comfort zone to experiment with new ideas or strategies. Taking calculated risks can lead to unexpected discoveries and innovations. This might involve launching a pilot project, adopting a new technology, or exploring unconventional partnerships. By doing so, you may uncover novel solutions and learn valuable lessons that could significantly benefit your personal brand or organization. Remember, innovation often stems from a willingness to venture into the unknown and challenge the status quo.

**Be sure to get
your free resources at
Uncopyableyou.com/resources**

NOTES

1. Gil Press, "Apple and Steve Jobs Steal From Xerox to Battle Big Brother IBM," *Forbes,* January 15, 2017; https://www .forbes.com/sites/gilpress/2017/01/15/steve-jobs-steals-from -xerox-to-battle-big-brother-ibm/?sh=42cf1f1012e0; accessed November 17, 2023.

2. For more information on Deming's benchmarking philosophy, read Chapter 6 in Steve Miller's book, *Uncopyable: How to Create an Unfair Advantage Over Your Competition,* published by Sound Wisdom.

3. This section is based on Steve Miller's book, *Stealing Genius: The Seven Levels of Adaptive Innovation,* published by Sound Wisdom.

5

HONOR YOUR PERSONAL VALUE, MISSION, AND RULES

- What do you stand for? (If you don't know, your target market won't know either.)

- What are you committed to doing, delivering, and denting the universe with? (Ditto.)

- What do you value, personally and professionally? What is your mission?

- Why do you do what you do? What is your purpose?

- What principles and operational standards support your purpose that you will never, ever compromise?

You can't create your own rules of competition until you create your own rules for yourself, which is a vitally important step, one that most people skip, minimize, or only pay lip service to. The personal rules you create affect everything. They must support your *purpose* in life.

Once you create your own rules for yourself, and are certain they align with your purpose, you face a critical choice: ***Will you walk the talk?***

YOU CAN'T CREATE YOUR OWN RULES OF COMPETITION UNTIL YOU CREATE YOUR OWN RULES FOR YOURSELF.

Once you walk the talk, and not before, you can *create your own myth*. (By the way, if the word "myth" still scares you after the brief explanation at the end of Chapter 3, it shouldn't. We'll explain more later in this chapter.)

Once you know, live, and are excited about sharing your myth, you can *refine your unique brand promise*—the commitment you make to the clearly defined group you serve that serves as the ultimate "Moose bait."

Once you know your brand promise with certainty, it's up to you to *align with it genuinely*. This is simple. It's not always easy. In fact, it's typically quite challenging. But it *is* simple—meaning it is always clear. You know when you are aligning with your own brand promise and when you aren't.

The following is one of our favorite examples of someone who did all of this on the way to creating and living a powerful personal brand.

Mr. Beast Finds His Purpose, His Voice, and His Moose

2014: Jimmy Donaldson, a North Carolina teenager known as Mr. Beast, launches his YouTube channel. Initially, it focuses on gaming content.

2016: The focus of the channel evolves. Mr. Beast gains attention, views, and subscribers by uploading videos of dramatic, high-impact donation challenges and philanthropic acts, such as tipping waitresses generously and donating to homeless shelters. In the process, he pioneers a new genre of YouTube video: *Interactions that make people's lives better* by means of expensive stunts. The genre explodes in popularity.

2017: Mr. Beast gets his first YouTube sponsorship offer—a potential $10,000 deal. Later, he tells the world that his first question, after receiving the offer was, *"How can I transform this money into something good?"* Not wanting to keep the money for himself, Jimmy tells the potential sponsor he will accept the deal on one condition: He gets to give the money away. The sponsor agrees.

2018: Mr. Beast's channel experiences significant growth as he continues to create videos centered on extreme challenges, donation drives, and philanthropy.

2019: Mr. Beast organizes a fundraiser to aid those affected by the devastating wildfires in Australia. Through his video "I Donated $100,000 To Random Twitch Streamers," he encourages his audience to contribute to the cause. The funds raised were donated to organizations involved in wildlife rescue and rehabilitation efforts. Mr. Beast's dedication to helping communities in times of crisis showcases his selflessness and desire to make a tangible difference in the lives of others. Mr. Beast reaches a major milestone of 20 million subscribers on YouTube, solidifying his position as one of the leading content creators on the platform.

2020: Mr. Beast launches "Team Trees," a campaign to plant 20 million trees worldwide. The initiative gains widespread support and successfully achieves its goal.

2021: Mr. Beast establishes the "Beast Philanthropy" organization, aiming to make a positive impact on a wide range of social issues. He continues to create engaging videos that combine entertainment with acts of generosity, inspiring millions of viewers around the world. Throughout this year, Mr. Beast's channel continues to experience exponential growth, amassing a massive following and becoming one of the most popular and influential channels on YouTube.

2022: Mr. Beast wins the Creator of the Year award at the Streamy Awards for the third straight year; he also wins the Favorite Male Creator award at the Nickelodeon Kids' Choice Awards for the second consecutive year.

2023: Time magazine names Mr. Beast as one of the world's 100 most influential people.

Think about:

- What is Mr. Beast's *purpose*?

- Who is his *Moose*?

- What is his *brand promise*?

- What is one personal rule he follows consistently?

Here are our answers to those questions. See how closely your responses matched up with ours.

What Is Mr. Beast's *Purpose?*

The compelling story of Mr. Beast's growth as an entrepreneur and a person leaves little doubt in our mind that his purpose is one he mentions often: *To leave the world a better place than he found it.* This simple, life-defining goal is our take on Mr. Beast's "Big Why." Look closely at his work, and you will see that this is the map he uses to chart his mission, and the standard he uses to evaluate his accomplishments. It's the ongoing, enduring quest that motivates him to do what he does.

NOTICE THAT A PURPOSE IS A PERSONAL GOAL SO BIG THAT IT CAN'T BE SIMPLY CHECKED OFF A TO-DO LIST.

Leaving the world a better place than he found it is what Mr. Beast is all about. Steve Jobs talked about wanting to leave a "dent in the universe" by empowering people with personal technology. Mr. Beast has a similarly inspiring, similarly unchanging aim—to improve the world.

Who Is Mr. Beast's *Moose?*

By this point in the book, we hope it is not a surprise to you to learn what we mean by that word "Moose." As a refresher, your Moose is the subsection of humanity you most want to engage with, learn more about, *and serve.*

It's no good saying that your aim is to engage with, learn more about, and serve *everyone on earth*—or everyone in the United States, or everyone in your metropolitan area. That's painting with way too broad a brush. One of the things we love about using Mr. Beast as an example is that even though he's emerged before even reaching the age of 30 as someone with global appeal and impact, his messaging is definitely targeted toward a very clearly defined chunk of the world. In other words, he doesn't pretend his videos will engage all groups equally. They're not designed to.

He chooses particular groups to communicate with, listen to, and serve. As of this writing, his Moose is males between the ages of 18 and 24. Does that mean none of his content appeals to females, or to people younger than 18 or older than 24? Of course not. But what becomes obvious from even a cursory review of his career is that males in that age group are who he is *aiming for,* and who he has reached most consistently.

What Is Mr. Beast's *Brand Promise?*

The brand promise is the commitment we make *and keep* to those we are aiming to reach with our messaging. We don't define the brand promise. The market does. It's what we tell them, directly or indirectly, that they are going to experience as a result of connecting with us—and after that, it's what they agree happens on a consistent basis. What matters is not so much what we say the brand promise is, but what our Moose *decides* has been promised and delivered.

With that key distinction in mind, we would submit that Mr. Beast's brand promise to his millions of YouTube viewers—the people who are the engine driving his whole enterprise—is *to leverage the power of social media to improve the world by making someone's life better in an entertaining and unforgettable way.*

Mr. Beast and his team have mastered the art of making viral videos. They've learned that one great way to do that is to design a dramatic stunt, usually one built around the idea of endurance, that culminates in a gift, something that makes someone's life a little better. (Example: "Last to Leave the Slime Pit Wins $20,000" racked up two million views.)

People have come to expect these kinds of videos from Mr. Beast and his team. Why? Because they've refined a brand promise that their Moose has come to rely on. They've made a commitment the market has learned to trust, a commitment that strengthens the bond of trust every time it's honored. And he and his team deliver consistently on that commitment. *How* consistently? Consistently enough to make Mr. Beast's channel among the most popular on the entire YouTube platform.

At last count, Mr. Beast had more than 250 million subscribers. It's estimated that he personally earned $54 million in 2021, including $32

NOTICE THAT THE MR. BEAST BRAND PROMISE RESTS SOLIDLY ON THE FOUNDATION OF HIS PURPOSE.

million from ads across his dozen-plus channels and $9 million from sponsored content. His studio is valued at roughly $1.5 billion, and his worth is "some $500 million."[1] By comparison, the Dreamworks studio is worth roughly $3.8 billion. But then Steven Spielberg, Jeffrey Katzenberg, and David Geffen got an earlier start on their project: 1994. And let's face it, although their movie studio may be worth twice as much as Mr. Beast's (right now), they're not as good at creating viral videos as Mr. Beast is.

What Is One Personal *Rule* Mr. Beast Follows?

A rule is a non-negotiable operating principle. The key to identifying and delivering on a brand promise is to get clear about the rules that support it—then follow those rules. It's evident to us that one of Mr. Beast's foundational rules is one he and his team express often: *Always ask, "How can I transform this money into something good?"*[2]

This is an operating principle that is not subject to debate in Mr. Beast's world. If it ever gets lost in the shuffle, he brings it back to the top of the conversation where it belongs. That's his role, both as a brand ambassador and a leader. *One of the signs of a valid personal Rule is that the leader—that's you, by the way—enjoys drawing attention to it!*

Now Here's Another Question for You: Who Is Mr. Beast's *Competition?*

As you may have guessed, that was a trick question. While Mr. Beast has plenty of imitators, in the most meaningful sense of the word

MR. BEAST HAS BUILT HIS OWN BOX AND CREATED HIS OWN UNIQUE RULES OF COMPETITION. THERE IS LITERALLY NO ONE WHO DOES PRECISELY WHAT HE DOES.

"competition," he *has* no competition. That's because he has built and defended a powerful personal brand that is legitimate to him as an individual, and that now defines his entire organization. That brand is solidly rooted in his personal values, beliefs, and rules. It is unique to him, which means his brand promise is unique to him.

What's the Point?

Why are we spending so much time on Mr. Beast? Because where he has landed is where you want to be. And because, in terms of personal branding strategy, you can do exactly what he has done.

Of course, whether you will end up doing it at the *scale* he has is a question we can't answer for you. And creating and sustaining a global brand may not be what you're after. (It's a lot of work.) But what we do know for sure is that, just like Mr. Beast, you can build your own box and create your own rules of competition...if.

If you know who you are, who you serve, what you offer them, and what you stand for.

The essence of being uncopyable, as we have said, lies in breaking free from the conventional practices and preconceptions of your competitors. These conventions typically involve benchmarking your competition and adhering to industry norms. As opposed to shattering them and creating something the competition hasn't even thought of, which is what people like Mr. Beast do. He invented his genre!

Conformity is the easy choice. Effective personal branding demands a very different approach. It demands that you *design, refine, and support a unique brand promise that is authentic to you as an individual.* The only way to do that is through a combination of experimentation and self-assessment. And that's exactly what we're challenging you to undertake in this chapter.

So get ready for that. Watch Mr. Beast on Youtube: youtube.com/@ MrBeast.

Your Hero's Journey

To differentiate yourself and escape the gravitational pull that leads to thinking and acting like everyone else, you must embark on your own hero's journey. You must summon the courage to *identify your inspiring personal purpose and the personal rules that will make it possible for you to keep pursuing that purpose **regardless the obstacles you encounter along the way.*** There will be many obstacles. But that's okay. When you are focusing on your purpose, you will find ways to transform those obstacles into opportunities.

These elements—your *Rules* and your *Purpose*—must be genuinely yours, not borrowed from others.[3] Only you can identify them. No focus group can do it for you. No consultant. No book like this. Yes, you read that right. We have come to the part of the book where (in the words of Shakespeare) "the patient must minister to himself."

The journey begins with *purpose.*

Your "Big Why" and Your Myth

Once you know what you stand for, what your purpose is, what your "Big Why" is, and what your personal rules are, you can refine your brand

YOUR MYTH IS REAL,
NOT PRETEND. IT'S
THE ONGOING,
CONTINUALLY
UPDATED REAL-LIFE
STORY OF YOU
FOLLOWING YOUR
RULES IN PURSUIT OF
YOUR BIG WHY.

promise. Your brand promise must be built on the foundation of your Big Why. It should embody your personal commitment to take that stand, pursue that Big Why and follow your rules without compromise.

If you should ever find yourself compromising your values (the core beliefs that support your Big Why) or your rules (the operating principles guide your pursuit of the goal identified by your Big Why) you will have a clear obligation: Acknowledge your lapse openly and without doubletalk...so you can fix it, quick.

This is called *walking your talk*. Walk your talk long enough, and authentically enough, and anecdotes will begin to appear in support of your Purpose, your value set, and your rules. Another term for these anecdotes is your *brand narrative*. We also use the word *myth* to describe the collection of narratives that, taken together, defines both you and your brand.

So: What is your Big Why? Is it to help children grow into mentally and physically healthy adults? Is it to inspire others with the power of the written word? Is it to create prosperity and self-reliance in the lives of people who would struggle without your help? Be prepared to spend some time with this question so you can come up with an answer that is uniquely yours.

Another Real-Life Example

We realize all of this may sound a bit abstract at first. So let's move on to the second big case study of this chapter, which will make these concepts more comprehensible and clearer.

We'd like to introduce you to...us.

Specifically we'd like to introduce you to one of your hosts, Steve, aka Kelly's Dad, aka the Marketing Gunslinger, who's walked the talk for decades now. He's a successful business owner who has hundreds of happy clients who have experienced increases in profit and substantial business growth, including a high percentage of repeat clients.

Steve's personal brand (that now includes and has been enhanced by the valuable addition of his wife, Kay, aka Muffler Mama) has grown into our company's brand, just as Mr. Beast's personal brand has grown into an organizational brand. What follows is our answer, as a company, to the four questions we asked you about Mr. Beast.

Our Purpose

Every single day, without exception, we touch at least one person in such a way as to improve their life, improve their world, and improve their business.

That's the purpose that gets us up early in the morning and keeps us up late at night. That's what we're here on earth to do. That's how we measure the success or failure of our projects: ***Did it touch someone? Did it improve their life, their world, and their business?*** And our company is the means by which we make that happen.

Our Moose

Our Moose is best described as "small B2B owners, marketers, and solo entrepreneurs who understand and accept our rules of engagement."

(More on our rules in a moment.) And oddly enough, since 1987, we have also attracted Fortune 1000 mega-corporations such as Proctor & Gamble, Boeing Commercial Airplane, Nordstrom, Starbucks, Caterpillar, Philips Electronics, Coca-Cola, and Halliburton, to name a few. Go figure.

Our Brand Promise

Organizations who work with us learn what it takes to become uncopyable and smarter, more effective marketers, and they learn that in a highly interactive, customized, educational, entertaining, and (dare we say it?) motivating way that empowers the rapid and successful implementation of big, game-changing ideas.

Notice that this brand promise is built solidly on the foundation of our purpose.

Our Rules, Part One

To be part of our business world, people must buy in to our operating principles—our rules. These are *non-negotiable prerequisites* for us doing what we do and adding the value that we add.

We are not kidding here. These things really are non-negotiable, as in, if you don't agree to this, we can't work with you. We post the rules on our website, and we only take on clients who explicitly agree to abide by those rules. *Once again: We do not paint with a broad brush.* We're not for everyone. Our Moose is not every company on earth.

Our Moose is those leaders of teams and organizations who understand the importance of standing out from the competition *and* are willing to sign off on our rules.

In a moment, you will read the client-facing rules that people who work with us have to sign off on *before* we agree to work with them. We're not reproducing them here because we believe they're right for you—they're not, they're right for us. We're sharing them with you now because we want you to see exactly what a unique and totally unapologetic set of operating principles looks, sounds, and feels like.

You already have one good, concise example of an operating principle that supports a powerful personal brand: Mr. Beast's rule, *"Always ask, How can I transform this money into something good?"* But simply memorizing someone else's rule isn't going to get you where you need to go! And one set of rules is not enough![4] That's why we want you to read our rules, too: So you can have another point of reference, and get a better sense of how to design, and live, your own rules.

Steve and Kay's Values and Rules

We are unique. We have rules and values that are not negotiable.

Our Values

We have a unique point of view.

Our clients engage us because we are committed to showing them *what's new, what's next, what's important, and what's the truth.* People do not hire us to tell them what they necessarily want to hear.

Business as usual is no longer an option.

We are allied with our clients. We inspire them to think and be different and be more successful (even if we have to drag them kicking and screaming).

We have a relentless desire to pursue novelty in what we do and how we do it. This keeps things lively and interesting.

We operate a no-spin zone.

IONSHO,[5] Conventional Wisdom is neither conventional, nor is it wisdom, and Common Sense is rarely Common Practice. If leaders in our industry are more interested in protecting Status Quo, than in taking the hard road, we will not hesitate to stand up and take the unpopular stance. That said, Steve has an edge. Kay isn't quite as edgy!

Our Rules

Rule of Fun

We believe that we tend to take ourselves and our work too seriously. Work should be serious fun.

Rule of Family

Our family is more important than you, and we expect your family to be more important than us. This means there may be times when we must choose between work and family.

Let's choose family.

Rule of RFPs

We do not do RFPs (Request for Proposals).

Rule of TRUST

We will work very hard to earn and keep your trust. We hope it goes both ways.

Rule of Hoops

We don't jump through hoops. Don't ask for details on our previous jobs. Our List of Clients and published books are an ample resumé.

Rule of Legalese

We do not do legal mumbo-jumbo.

Rule of Mutual Respect

We are not working *for* you. We are working *with* you, therefore we treat each other equally and with respect. If you call or email, for example, you expect a timely response. You will get it. We expect the same treatment in return.

Rule of No Ties

Steve does not wear a tie. Kay, apparently, never has.

Rule of Value

We are not cheap. Our fees are neither based on time nor travel. They are based on the ultimate value of our participation, as well as our own unique experiences (professional and personal), and education. If you are looking for cheap, we are happy to suggest less-experienced speakers and consultants.

Steve's Rule of Travel

Steve doesn't fly coach. In the years since airlines started frequent flyer programs, he has accumulated 6,178,546 miles on American Airlines alone (as of 09/01/2023). This is over 12,300 hours in the air, which does not include time on the ground, delayed or cancelled flights, time in the airports, travel to and from the airports, or bedbugs. In order for him to be fully productive, physically rested, and mentally fresh for you, he flies first class. (If you can even get him in the air anymore.)

Kay's Rule of Travel

Kay is much more flexible than Steve. You should pick Kay.

Our Rules, Part Two

When we show our list of rules to people, and tell them it's time to create a list of original personal rules of their own—not an identical list, but one that does the same basic job our rules do—we typically hear some variation on this question:

Isn't that a bit aggressive?

Our answer is always the same: We prefer the word *direct.* And yes. What you just read is direct. Why? Because it has to be.

There is no way to create an effective personal brand that is tentative, familiar, and conformist. There is no way to set and live your values, your rules, and your purpose that is indirect and apologetic. ***You are who you are***. What you stand for is what you stand for. What you believe is what you believe. Your rules of engagement are your rules of your engagement.

If you aren't willing to figure out what you stand for, what you are committed to, and how you deliver value—if you are not willing to express all of that directly, then there's no way your target audience will ever hear, see, or feel the difference you can make in their world. And there's no way you will ever stand out from the competition.

What you just read is, of course, framed in such a way as to match up with who *we* are. Your job is not to imitate our voice, or anyone else's. Your job is to identify your own rules of engagement, and then communicate them (online and in person and via every conceivable touch point) in *your* voice.

To do that, you have to understand your personal narrative.

And to do that, *you have to live (not just write) your rules*. As we like to call it, *live your myth*.

How Your Rules Help You Build Your Brand Narrative

There are two classic mistakes people make when it comes to understanding their own brand narrative:

- The first mistake is imagining that their narrative has nothing to do with their operating principles. In most cases, they don't even know what their operating principles are, so they try to create their brand narrative before they figure out what it is they stand for and will not compromise.

- The second classic mistake is imagining that there's only one narrative: They fixate on a single plotline, and they ignore the reality that *multiple* powerful brand narratives will emerge in their world on a consistent basis once they know what they stand for. And that's great. The more narratives you have that support your personal brand, the better!

Every effective brand narrative comes from you living your principles, even in—especially in—the face of profound opposition or difficulty. Once you realize that, it will become obvious to you that brand narratives are everywhere, assuming you know your rules and are unwilling to compromise those rules. All you have to do is notice the situations where you are willing to take a stand.

The following is an example of what we mean by this. A condensed brand narrative that connects in a powerful way to Steve is this example, which we have been sharing for decades:

> *Steve is a bestselling author, a professional speaker, and business advisor, known for his edgy, no-spin-zone style. He's the son of the co-inventor of the 8-track, he's played on the PGA Tour, worked in the copper mines of Arizona, managed a roller skating rink, and even worked in Hollywood (all of which means he's basically unemployable). He founded The Adventure LLC in 1984 and has worked as a marketing consultant with some of the most prominent brands in America. (He prefers working with much smaller businesses*

because he can actually make an impact.) He doesn't have an MBA and jokes that he "majored in electives."

Since starting The Adventure, he's been committed to the philosophies he's developed. He truly is "Uncopyable" (according to Kay and many others)! He's also a deep thinker, voracious reader, and dedicated learner. His mission is to be uniquely valuable to his clients—to get them thinking in new ways that explode their opportunities for success. From teaching them the art of "Stealing Genius" to the concept of "Building Your Own Box," he's dedicated to helping clients make more money. For Steve, it goes beyond business. He gets the most satisfaction when he hears from former clients—often many years later—that Steve made a life-changing impact on their business, and on them personally.

Here's Kay's condensed brand narrative:

Kay is an author, consultant, and speaker. She's also a people person who loves to spend time talking, listening and usually cracking a joke or two. She grew up with an entrepreneurial spirit and sold a variety of products all with something in common—which is pretty easy to spot: Kay's Kandy, Kay's Kandles, Kay's Kits, etc. After high school, she took her college years seriously and was committed to finishing on time. Especially since her parents were only paying half. Her dad sent her off with the warning: "Four years only!" Even though she was known as a bit of a partier, she graduated Summa Cum Laude. And yes, she finished a little less than four years later. She earned a business degree, but her psychology classes were some of her favorites; in fact, she fell just short of a psychology minor.

She loves to get to know people and understand them. Her mission when working with a client: "I want them to succeed." She's dedicated to helping them and prioritizes the relationship. In fact, she considers many of them friends. Kay fully embraces the Uncopyable philosophy as a whole new way of thinking. She's passionate about sharing this life-changing perspective. She loves watching "the ones who get it" and take a deep dive into who they are, what they stand for, and how they can use their own uncopyable gifts to impact their world.

Our mini-narrative lands the message:

This is what "unique" and "point of view" mean to us. If you decide to work with us, you'll be getting an unconventional perspective that you will get literally nowhere else, a perspective that's rooted in an unconventional work history. If Steve's background is not what you're looking for, and you decide there's no match here, that's fine. Just know that this unique experience, and the perspective arising from it, is where our value comes from.

Can you begin to see how the narratives and the rules work hand in hand? You really can't have one without the other. If you walk the talk, you're eventually going to run up against some friction; how you deal with that friction is usually pretty good "material." The narratives emerge almost automatically.

Is everybody going to connect with your narrative? Of course not. That's the point. The narrative should bring some people closer into your orbit and let others know that it's okay if you're not their cup of tea.

> *Having a clear narrative helps you change your mental focus from "searching for business, any business" to "delivering high value to and receiving fair compensation from, the target market." YOU ARE NOT FOR EVERYONE, AND THAT IS OKAY!*

The following is another powerful brand narrative that came about because we walked our myth. It's one we make a point of sharing with prospective new clients.

> *It doesn't happen often, because we're pretty careful in our selection process, but every once in a while we will fire a client for not following the rules. Sometimes clients are surprised by this; they'll say things such as, "You mean to tell me you're just walking away from X dollars?" And the truth of the matter is, we've walked away from very, very large sums of money because people would not follow the rules.*
>
> *Years ago, we had a client who was a new senior executive at a major corporation. She'd replaced our original client who left for a bigger position. It was a big engagement worth a lot of money. Let's call her Client A. Now, Client A apparently didn't like the fact she inherited us, and she tried getting us to jump through some hoops we hadn't signed up for. Instead of creating a big emotional scene on the phone*

when it continued to happen, we opted to send her a Federal Express package with a formal letter informing her that she'd been fired.

As it happened, she received that package while she was heading out the door to have dinner with another client of ours, we'll call him Client B. At dinner Client A read the letter informing her of her termination and her face went red. How do we know? Because Client B could hardly wait to get out of the restaurant and call us to give us a blow-by-blow account of the meltdown. That call was one of the high points of our year.

Once you have enough clarity on your rules to live them without compromise, your brand narrative becomes clearer. Once your narrative is clear, you get better at sharing it with your target audience. The better you get at sharing your brand narrative with your target audience, the better you will be at refining your brand promise so that it resonates with them.

Internal Versus External Rules

What we've shared with you thus far about our own rules are the ones we put on our website—the client-facing rules. These are external rules, and of course they're crucial to formulate and share because they help shape people's understanding of both our narrative and our brand promise. But they're not the only types of important rules. There are also internal rules, rules that the client may never see or come into contact with, but that are just as important as the ones you share with the outside world. Like your external rules, your internal rules need to be built on the foundation of your purpose.

The following are two examples of internal rules that have become central to our brand.

1. The Rule of Vicious Productivity

Some tasks that have an impact on the client experience can be completed by paying someone $20 an hour to do the work. Other tasks have an exponentially larger impact on the client experience, but can only be completed by someone paying *us* $500 an hour to do the work. We are therefore vicious about protecting what we call our $500-an-hour time. The word "vicious" doesn't suggest that we're mean. It just means we're adamant about farming out $20-an-hour work, so we can focus on $500-an-hour-work. We are serious when it comes to defending the time we have blocked out for $500-an-hour work. We are willing to go to great lengths in our defense of productivity.

Wouldn't you?

2. The Rule of Impact Management

We do not do *time* management. We do *impact* management. We constantly ask ourselves, *Am I working on something that will help us to move forward on the attainment of a big goal?* If the answer is no, we reprioritize. Reprioritizing may mean farming out $20-an-hour work. (See the Rule of Vicious Productivity.)

Successful personal branding means understanding that your brand has unique internal and external

rules, identifying those rules, and following them when it would be easier not to.

We call standing up for your rules without compromise *living your myth.* Living your myth is how you communicate your brand to the wider world. Each and every time you live your myth, your brand gains more power to make a deep and memorable impression on your target audience. Each and every time you live your myth, you get clearer about your brand promise and about the value you deliver—which means your target audience becomes clearer about your brand promise and the value you deliver.

You are unique. You have a unique purpose and unique rules that are not negotiable. Your job now is really quite simple, though it is certainly not easy: Identify those rules, live them consistently, use them to refine your personal brand promise, and once the promise is refined, to share that promise in lots of different ways with people in your target audience— your Moose—who can take you up on it.

Full Disclosure

The Rules page on our website is the second-most visited page. It's also the most copied. Don't do that. Use our rules as inspiration.

Most people *don't* take the time to fully develop and widely share their purpose or their rules. The reason for this failure is pretty simple:

Identifying these things takes time, and living in accordance with them takes courage. In this chapter, we challenge you to invest that time and find that courage.

Coming up with a list that encompasses your personal purpose and your personal rules is not an overnight assignment. It's not easy. But it's essential. And if you've made it this far in the book with us, we're guessing you get that.

Sometimes when we outline what needs to happen next, people tell us they have a lot of other things going on in their lives. They tell us they're not sure how to get started. They tell us they're already holding down a full-time job (or a bunch of side gigs) and they aren't sure they have the bandwidth to complete this work. But you know what? When it comes right down to it, the people who are serious about building and defending a strong personal brand set priorities, start anywhere, and find the bandwidth. And we're betting you are that kind of person.

You can do this.

We want to be straight with you here. It's going to take you some serious time to get this next part right, assuming you are putting an hour or so into it every day. And here's the truth not everyone is ready to hear: You can't skip the assignment you'll find at the end of this chapter if you expect to build and support a powerful personal brand.

Two Good Reasons

There are two good reasons to set aside the time and energy required to complete the assignment you are about to read.

SET YOUR PURPOSE
....
AND YOUR RULES—
....
AND REFINE YOUR
....
PERSONAL BRAND
....
PROMISE.
....

First, doing this will empower you to create, and live, a brand promise that helps people in your target audience to *trust you.*

Once you are crystal-clear on that brand promise, you will get better and better at fulfilling that promise—thereby not just meeting but exceeding the expectations you set. People who set and meet expectations earn trust.

Second, doing this will make it easier for people in your target audience to *remember you*.

Now that you've reached the end of this chapter, it's highly unlikely that you will ever forget Mr. Beast, what he stands for, and what makes him unique. (Think: *Make the world a better place.*) And we're going to go out on a limb and predict that you will also remember Steve and Kay, what *they* stands for, what makes *them* unique (Think: *What's new, what's next, what's important, and what's the truth,* and *we're not cheap.*) If you believe that being that memorable to your chosen audience will make a difference to you, personally and professionally—and make no mistake, it will—then you are ready for the next steps.

Refine Your Personal Brand Promise

Complete the sentences, and then share your work with someone who loves you enough to tell you the truth when you ask them, "Is this me?"

1. My purpose in life, the reason I'm here on earth is:

(Your purpose is not something that can be crossed off a to-do list. Purpose typically connects to some form of service.)

2. The specific ways that my purpose in life connects directly to quantifiable *value* I deliver to my target audience is:

List as many as possible.

3. My *internal* rules are:

List as many as possible. Remember that a rule is something you will take a stand for, even when it would be easier not to.

4. My *external* rules are:

Again list as many as possible. Remember that a rule is something you will take a stand for, even when it would be easier not to.

5. Knowing what you now know about your purpose and your rules, how would you refine your personal brand promise?

What words would you now use to share that promise with a prospective client/customer? What personal brand narratives have emerged for you? How would you share those stories with a prospective client/customer?

**Be sure to get
your free resources at
Uncopyableyou.com/resources**

NOTES

1. Chloe Sorvina, "Could MrBeast Be The First YouTuber Billionaire?" *Forbes,* November 30, 2022; https://www.forbes .com/sites/chloesorvino/2022/11/30/could-mrbeast-be-the -first-youtuber-billionaire/?sh=1788d774191a; accessed November 18, 2023.

2. Of course, Mr. Beast has *multiple* rules that support his purpose. We're not examining them all here because if we did, the longest chapter in this book would be even longer than it already is. A particularly important rule that we've picked up from the interviews he's given is one we happen to share with him: Work should be fun. Yes, it's important. Yes, it's serious. But if work is not also enjoyable, something is missing.

3. You may also choose to identify personal values, beliefs that support your rules. Values are the truths you hold as self-evident. Values are optional in the process we are sharing with you here, but rules are essential.

4. Until you design and live your own operating principles, your personal branding will be incomplete, because it will be unconnected to anything real in your world.

5. In Our Not So Humble Opinion ¯_(ツ)_/¯

6

CREATE ANCHORS AND TRIGGERS TO EVOKE YOUR PERSONAL BRAND AND PROMISE

Learn how to design and execute a carefully crafted visual plan that builds strong positive associations in your target market by using time-tested principles of perception, psychology, and persuasion.

Years ago, Steve was preparing to deliver a speech at a large conference taking place at the Dallas Anatole Hotel. The Anatole is a huge complex. Thanks to its size and layout, it is capable of hosting multiple major events simultaneously. On this particular day, Steve saw that the annual convention of Mary Kay Cosmetics was taking place on the other side of the facility. Steve was (and is) a curious guy, so he decided to take a break and walk over to the side of the complex where Mary Kay's event was being held. He wanted to see what was going on.

He found himself engulfed in a sea of near-total *pink*. Hundreds of well-dressed, well-heeled, well-cosmeticked women were rushing through the hotel lobby and hallways. Virtually every one of these women were wearing some kind of pink attire. Most were wearing pink blazers with massive pink ribbons lining the front. (Steve later learned these were recognition ribbons.) Some of the women sported so many ribbons that they had pink running all the way down their sleeves!

He could hardly believe his eyes. It was like some kind of cult. He asked himself, *What in the world is going on here?*

What was going on was a master class in anchoring and triggering in support of a brand promise. And the women moving busily through the Anatole were proof of concept for Mary Kay Ash (1918-1921), a gifted entrepreneur and a master of both personal and organizational branding.

Some background on the remarkable Mary Kay Ash is in order before we go any further.

Disappointed after being overlooked for a promotion in favor of a male colleague whom she had trained, Ash made the decision to retire in 1963. Her retirement plan initially involved writing a book aimed at assisting women in the business world. However, her book gradually transformed into a comprehensive business plan for her ideal company. During the summer of 1963, Mary Kay Ash and her newlywed husband, George Hallenbeck, envisioned the establishment of a new kind of cosmetics company. Tragically, George passed away from a heart attack just one month before they were set to launch Beauty by Mary Kay, as the company was originally named.

Undeterred by the loss, and driven by her entrepreneurial spirit, Ash continued with her plan to launch the new company on the same schedule. At the age of 45, she received a $5,000 investment from her eldest son, Ben Rogers Jr., and enlisted the support of her younger son, Richard Rogers, to take over her late husband's role. The company commenced its operations in a modest 500-square-foot storefront in Dallas.

Initially, nine saleswomen were recruited to work, using the "house party" model Ash adapted from other companies like Stanley and Tupperware. In this approach, a Mary Kay representative invited friends over for complimentary facials, eventually presenting the products for sale. The company experienced significant profits, achieving double-digit growth year after year. And believe it or not, that growth would not have been possible without Mary Kay Ash's fixation on the color pink.

Color as an Anchor Trigger

Pink was an integral part of Mary Kay Ash's world, permeating every aspect of her business. She made pink synonymous with her brand, and with its emotionally potent promise of confidence, beauty, and empowerment. That was a promise she made and kept—not just to customers, but also to her army of high-achieving salespeople. And yes, they were mostly women.

The deliberate association between Mary Kay Ash's company and the color pink was no accident. Every pink touchpoint served a purpose: To establish a bond in the observer's mind. This intentional branding approach created an anchor activated upon encountering a trigger. As an observer, once you witnessed the color pink in any context, regardless of the source or reason, such as spotting it on a woman's dress, your thoughts naturally gravitated toward Mary Kay

Ash Cosmetics and its brand promise of beauty, empowerment, and confidence. This method of back-of-mind branding aimed to generate top-of-mind awareness by establishing strong positive subconscious associations.

Ash had made the fateful decision to link her personal brand to pink back when she introduced her very first product, the Basic Treatment Set. By the time Steve saw her and her organization in action, pink was both an expression of her personal brand and an important organizational brand statement, one that had extended to every conceivable touchpoint associated with Mary Kay Cosmetics, both internally and externally.

While some might perceive Ash's relentless dedication to the color pink as a bit extreme, as a marketing choice that came to border on obsession, we think it was a shrewd business decision. Her obsession made Mary Kay Ash a powerful role model for her sales team. Today, she remains a powerful role model for anyone launching a personal branding campaign.

Start with collateral, and notice what Ash did with hers: She meticulously crafted her product packaging strategy around the color pink, designing marketing materials, company stationery, and envelopes to reflect this signature hue. And of course her obsession with pink went well beyond products and stationery. Her choice of a pink Cadillac as her personal vehicle, and her practice of leasing pink Cadillacs to high-performing "beauty consultants," further solidified the connection between the color pink and her brand. The iconic pink Cadillac is still synonymous with her company and her brand, years after her passing. As obsessions go, color and imagery seems to us like one that's worth pursuing if you're interested in personal and professional branding.

For most women, the last bit of applause they received was when they graduated from high school or college.... When a Mary Kay Sales Director drives a pink Cadillac, she is recognized as a person who has done an outstanding job. It signifies that she is very important to our organization.

—Mary Kay Ash

That famous pink Cadillac brings us to an extremely important point about Mary Kay's personal and organizational brand strategy. We've already pointed out that she found ways to subliminally link the color pink to brand messaging emphasizing beauty, empowerment, and confidence. That was for her customers. No doubt about it, female buyers of cosmetic products constituted one important part of Mary Kay's target audience—her Moose. But she also had another audience—another group of people she wanted to reach with a slightly different, but complementary, brand message. Can you figure out who that second Moose was?

Evoking Ideas

Of course. It was those women Steve saw rushing to and fro at the Anatole Hotel—the "beauty consultants" who sold Mary Kay products. For them, the color pink carried a special, deeper set of associations. Mary Kay Ash devoted years of her life to making certain that, for people on her sales team, for people *aspiring* to become part of her sales team, for people who *interacted* with anyone on her sales team, the color pink not only symbolized beauty, confidence, and empowerment—it also evoked the ideas of *entrepreneurial spirit, prosperity,* and *large-scale financial success.*

That's the message the famous pink Cadillac sent (and continues to send) to women: *You can achieve financial success, and you can do it on your own, just like Mary Kay did.* You only get to drive a pink Cadillac when you reach the upper tier of revenue production as a Mary Kay consultant. Every time one of those top producers drove around town in that pink Caddy, *she was sending a brand message.* And by the way, that's also the message Mary Kay Ash's 30-room mansion—predominantly pink, inside and out—sent and reinforced, too. Yes, as the founder and leader of the company, Mary Kay herself had to back that message up with action, effective strategy, and leadership. The record is unequivocal—she did just that. In the most recent year for which figures are available, 2022, Mary Kay Cosmetics cleared $2.5 billion in revenues, and the products are sold in more than 40 markets worldwide, with a global independent sales force exceeding 3.5 million.[1]

This is why we still say that the pink Cadillac remains a pretty powerful success story—not just for the company, but for the principles of anchoring and triggering that Mary Kay Ash pioneered, starting in the early 1960s. (They inspired us personally, as you'll learn a little later in this chapter.) She used the color pink as an anchor to send powerful, carefully chosen brand messages to her target audience, messages that, like the color pink she made her own, supported a powerful personal mission, a purpose. That purpose outlived her, as the very best purposes do, and it continues to inspire people to this day. Her mission was simple, and you can find it framed in pink on the website of the company she founded.

Mary Kay's mission is unchanged: To enrich the lives of women and their families.

CONNECT YOUR MISSION AND YOUR BRAND PROMISE TO THE WORLD YOUR MOOSE INHABITS.

What Mary Kay Ash did, in a stroke of personal branding genius, was to connect her mission—enriching the lives of women and their families—to the visual world her audience inhabited. She did that in a compelling, impossible-to-forget way, by coordinating anything and everything her company did in support of her mission with the color pink, to an almost obsessive degree. What she did when she connected the Mary Kay brand with the color pink is known as *anchoring*. Then whenever people were re-exposed to the anchor (pink), as evidenced by the website, a product, a representative's outfit, or even their car, that's known as a *trigger*.

And we decided to follow her example by setting anchors and eliciting triggers ourselves. We started where she started, by selecting a color. And our strategic use of color, which fuses orange with our purpose and our brand promise, serves as the case study for this powerful personal branding, best practice.

You'll recall our purpose: ***Each day, without exception, we are here to touch at least one person in such a way as to improve their life, improve their world, and improve their business***.

And you'll recall the brand promise they've built on the foundation of that purpose:

Organizations and people who work with us learn what it takes to become uncopyable, and they learn that in a highly interactive, customized, educational, entertaining, and motivating way that empowers the rapid and successful implementation of big, game-changing ideas.

So perhaps now you're wondering: How did we connect color to those elements? How did we fuse our purpose and our brand promise with the visual world our Moose inhabits?

Glad you asked.

After that trip to Texas where Steve noticed all the Mary Kay pink, he decided he wanted to inspire the same level of awareness and attachment in his world that Mary Kay Ash had created in hers. He decided that, like Mary Kay's business, our company needed a signature color, a color that would permeate virtually every interaction and every touch point, making a lasting impression on anyone who had anything to do with us. But how would we select the perfect color? And which one had the most potential to attract interest and inspire action?

Steve pondered this question and came up with an unconventional idea. He cut out a multitude of colors, creating a vibrant mosaic of swaths. He laid them out meticulously on the floor. With a sense of curiosity, he enlisted the help of our then-two-year-old daughter, Kelly. He asked her which she liked. He watched as Kelly's tiny finger pointed toward a particular shade. It was orange.

Days later, Steve repeated the experiment, wondering if the results would remain the same. He presented the array of colors once again, observing Kelly's gaze shifting from one shade to another. Without any hesitation, she chose orange for the second time. It was a resounding confirmation. Steve decided that if our two-year-old daughter consistently gravitated toward orange, there must be something inherently captivating about it. On that day, orange officially became Steve's (and eventually Kay's) color and the company's color emblem of brand identity. And it has remained so for three decades.

Prior to this, we had been using a mishmash of colors. We had different hues scattered across business cards, advertisements, brochures, envelopes, and stationery. There was no unifying element, and no consistent visual brand message. Now, everything changed. Orange became the defining visual characteristic of our interaction with each client and each prospective client.

Every business card handed out, every letter mailed, and every piece of marketing collateral distributed was graphically built around orange as the dominant color. Steve started driving an orange Jeep. And he made sure to wear at least one highly visible item of orange clothing to each and every business event—a practice we both continue to this day. When it came time to launch a website, Steve told the designer to build it around the color orange. Both of our books, Steve's *Uncopyable* and *Stealing Genius* and Kay's *Uncopyable Sales Secrets,* and now this one, have orange covers. In short, *every time we do anything to fulfill the mission and carry out the brand promise, we make sure orange is visually prominent.*

And the results have been remarkable. When the people we target—the people we work with, our Moose—see orange, they think of us, our purpose, and our brand promise. Why? Because of the *anchor* we have built with the color orange. When they see the color orange, either from some kind of communication with us or from some other source, that *triggers* them to experience or re-experience positive past interactions with us. It reminds them of being *Uncopyable.* It reminds them of Kay and Steve. And they *engage.* This, then, is the formula not just for Mary Kay Ash, but for us, and now for you, too:

Anchor + Trigger = Engage

In our world, orange stands for something specific. It stands for any initiative, big or small, undertaken in such a way as to improve someone's life. It stands for a promise we make to someone in our target audience that lines up with that mission, a promise that is fulfilled. And it stands for our commitment to find ways to deliver *continuous* value to all the Moose we manage to reach, whether they're clients or not.

That may seem like an absurdly high place to set the bar, but it works for us.

We create *anchors* in the world every time we fulfill any part of our brand promise with an action *(any* action!) that supports our mission, and we do that by linking everything good we do with the color orange. As a result, our Moose gets triggered by orange and engages or re-engages with us—not just by hiring us, but in many, many other ways as well!

Picture a Moose in the forest. Its nostrils twitch; it has smelled some Moose bait. Now picture it stalking through the forest toward the source of that scent; picture it approaching a Moose-bait dispenser that's colored bright orange. Now picture the Moose pushing a prominent button on that Moose-bait dispenser with its massive antlers, receiving a piece of delicious Moose bait, eating it, and pushing the button again. Eventually, the Moose gets full and wanders away. But a week, a month, or a year later, the Moose spots a tiny flash of orange in the forest. What happens? The Moose moves toward it. It picks up speed, and pretty soon it's running toward the orange at full speed. It wants to push that button again.

That's what we're all about—getting the Moose to nudge that button multiple times, so we can fulfill our brand promise in some way to every, and yes, we mean *every* Moose who comes in contact with us, no matter what form that contact may take. This engagement and re-engagement cycle has happened more times than we can count over the years; and as we hope you've picked up on by now, it doesn't just happen with clients.

The following is one of our favorite examples of the cycle happening with someone who *became* a client. This is not only proof of this chapter's core concept, but also one of our key brand narratives!

"Mattress Mack"

Jim McIngvale, also known as "Mattress Mack," hails from Houston, Texas. He is famous in his market for his flourishing furniture stores, his popular radio station, and his unwavering commitment to the community in which he lives. Notably, during challenging times including Hurricane Harvey in 2017, Tropical Storm Imelda in 2019, and the 2021 Texas power crisis, McIngvale generously opened the doors of his Gallery Furniture stores to provide shelter for displaced Texans seeking refuge from the elements. His compassionate actions garnered widespread praise and admiration, all of it well-deserved.

For several years we've made a practice of sending autographed books to people we admire. If we read or hear about someone who has done something extraordinary, maybe even uncopyable, we wrap up copies of our books, pack them in an orange box, write a personal note, and send them as a gift. Just something cool we like to do. Sometimes we get a thank you, most of the time we don't hear anything. That's okay.

In 2017, Kay saw a story about McIngvale's generosity in sheltering residents who'd been displaced by Hurricane Harvey. When she told Steve, they both decided he was someone they wanted to connect with. They sent him a *shock and awe package*—an orange box filled with orange goodies—an orange umbrella, an orange journal, orange sunglasses, orange shoelaces, an orange pen, an orange highlighter, and an orange shotglass. Besides these, the accompanying letterhead, business cards, and bookmarks were also designed to highlight the color orange. Also included was an autographed copy of Steve's book, *Uncopyable*. Like all of Steve and Kay's books, *Uncopyable* has a bright orange cover.

We now fill in some of the blanks in the story with what Jim McIn-gvale told us *after* he became a client of ours. He received the package, opened it, saw the book with the powerful title and the bright orange cover, was intrigued, flipped to the first page of *Uncopyable*, and read it cover to cover. When he was done, he made a mental note: *I want to work with this guy; I need to call Steve so we can talk.* Then, as is often the case with leaders of organizations, he got sidetracked. Something important came up, and he forgot all about calling Steve.

Several months passed until the day came when Steve received a call from Jim McIngvale himself. Curious about the impetus behind the unexpected call, Steve asked about it and listened as McIngvale explained the chain of events that had led to their conversation.

The previous night, McIngvale had attended the Opening Day game of the Houston Astros baseball team. As the team stormed onto the field in the top of the first inning, the vivid orange color dominating their jerseys caught McIngvale's attention. This sight *triggered* his memory of the orange book he had received. Suddenly he remembered he had meant to call Steve about working together, but became busy like we all do from time to time. The sight of the Houston Astros' uniforms served as a reminder that he had a call to make.

The next morning he called Steve directly. And that phone call culminated in a major consulting assignment.

So here's what we want you to notice. Jim McIngvale smelled some Moose bait, pushed the button on the dispenser, devoured the Moose bait, then got distracted, as Moose sometimes do. Months later, he spotted a tiny flash of orange, then ran at full speed toward it so he could push that button again.

Steve's choice to utilize the color orange in his book's presentation and in the supporting materials created an anchor—a distinct association that resonated with McIngvale. The triggering effect of seeing the Houston Astros adorned in orange jerseys prompted memory and engagement, and a meaningful long-term professional relationship. By aligning visual brand elements strategically, Steve not only captured the attention of a key decision maker, he also evoked a powerful connection with a past positive experience (reading Steve's book) that propelled a new business relationship forward.

This true story, one of dozens we could share, illustrates the potency of anchoring and triggering. More than one BFF (that's what we call our clients and followers!) has said, "I can't see the color orange without thinking of you!"

But the Story Doesn't Stop There!

You'll recall that we mentioned, a little earlier in this chapter, that we are committed to finding ways to deliver *continuous* value to *all* the Moose we manage to reach, whether they're clients or not. That commitment is playing out *right now, as you read these words!*

We don't just use the color orange to *initiate* interactions with Moose. We use it to *sustain, reinforce,* and *expand* interactions—not just with people who have paid to secure our services, but with *everyone* in our target audience. That means that when a former client sees the color orange *in any setting,* be it the cover of this book, or a sport's team's uniform, or an orange coffee cup someone happens to pull out of the dishwasher, *they are pulled back into the memory of their last interaction with us.* If that interaction fulfilled our brand promise, the color orange inspires them to *implement whatever best practice they learned about in that interaction*—and who knows, maybe reach out to us for another piece of Moose bait!

And guess what? Our clients are not the only ones who see the color orange and are pulled back into that memory of a positive experience. *You, too, are now anchored to the color orange!* As a reader of this book, you are now officially a BFF and part of this story. From this moment forward, every time you see the color orange, *you* have the opportunity to turn that anchor into a trigger. How? By *reinforcing and/or implementing something important you've learned between the covers of this book.* For instance, by being clear about and executing your brand promise; by stealing genius; by setting up anchors and triggers of your own; and by getting your own Moose to spot *your* Moose dispenser and pick up the scent of *your* Moose bait as it wanders through the forest! The list goes on and on; and every time you see the color orange, you're going to have what we like to call a "Jim McIngvale Moment"!

> *Every time someone who has worked with us sees the color orange, exposure to that color serves as a trigger. That trigger* **reinforces and awakens the big takeaways from that work we've done together.** *When someone special—one of our clients, or one of the people who has read our stuff or seen our videos or heard us on a podcast—sees the color orange, a mental connection begins at the subconscious level of the brain and sometimes fires off at the conscious level. That question sounds like this: Hey,* **is this an opportunity to be uncopyable?**

You're now one of those special people. And the next time *you* see an orange coffee cup or a billboard that prominently features the color orange or who knows, maybe just an orange, we want that powerful question about being uncopyable that you just read to transition into another powerful question: *How can I use anchors and triggers to reinforce and reawaken the experience my clients and customers have when they work with me?*

Anchoring and Triggering 102

What you've just read—and we hope considered deeply enough to make you eager to implement your own anchors-and-triggers process—could be described as a course in your Uncopyable curriculum that shows up in the catalog as *Anchoring and Triggering 101*. It's basically the foundation of what we've been sharing, testing, refining, and proving out for decades now with clients and readers who are new to these principles.

What you're *about* to read is what we share with people who are ready, willing, and able to take these ideas to the next level. Is that you? Given how far you've come in the book, we're thinking it is you. (You thought we didn't notice all that hard work you've been doing? Wrong. We did!)

The five powerful concepts you're about to learn, taken together, constitute *Anchoring and Triggering 102*. Once you've internalized and begun to execute the stuff in 101, you can build on it by internalizing and executing the following five big ideas.

Big Idea #1: Move Beyond Color

Set at least three anchors. One of them should be a word or phrase that summarizes exactly what you are all about. Choosing a color (or combination of colors) to create anchors is fine, but it's not the whole job. If possible, look for a memorable word or phrase that perfectly captures what you stand for, and does so in a way that separates you quickly and decisively from all potential competitors. That phrase has to encapsulate and support your values, your mission, and your brand promise, so it's worth taking the time to get right.

As a perfect example of a motto that captures the essence of both a personal and an organizational brand, we always come back to Steve Jobs's famous two-word summary: *Think different.* Innovation is what Jobs himself was all about, it was what the company he co-founded was all about, and it's what he appealed to as the organizational compass-point when, after leaving Apple, he returned during a period of crisis for a now-legendary second stint as CEO beginning in 1998. The core message was always the same: *Think different!* Here's what Jobs said to his inner circle at a 1997 meeting, while he was still technically an "advisor" to senior leadership, an "advisor" busy engineering the historic turnaround that would come to define both him and the company:

> *This is a very complicated world, a very noisy world, and we're not going to get a chance to get people to remember much about us. No company is. And so we have to be really clear on what we want them to know about us. Now, Apple, fortunately, is one of the half-dozen best brands in the whole world. We're right up there with Nike, Disney,*

Coke, Sony—Apple is one of the greats of the greats, not just in this country but all around the globe. But even a great brand needs investments and caring if it's going to retain its relevance and vitality. And the Apple brand has clearly suffered from neglect in this area in the last few years. And we need to bring it back. The way to do that is not to talk about speeds and feeds. It's not to talk about megahertz. It's not to talk about why we're better than Windows.... Our customers want to know, Who is Apple? And what do we stand for? Where do we fit in this world? And what we're about isn't making boxes for people to get their jobs done, although we do that well. We do that better than almost anybody.... But Apple's about something more than that. Apple, at the core, its core value, is that we believe that people with passion can change the world for the better. That's what we believe... and that those people who are crazy enough to think they can change the world are the ones that actually do.

So, take Steve Jobs as an example. Take "Think different" as an example. Come up with an equally distinctive, equally memorable phrase that tells your customers who you are, what you stand for, and what you believe. In the end, what people will remember is what you make clear to them that you value enough to take a stand for.

Note: It could be longer, such as Katie's phrase: *I want every prospective client I meet to have a better life than they had before they met me. I'm going to make sure that every person I meet is better off having met me than they would have been not having met me.*

We've emphasized what we've done with the color orange because we've found that is the part of the curriculum people can get their head around most easily and quickly. In the real world, we coach our clients to create at least *three* interlocking, compatible, complementary anchors that define and amplify their personal and/or organizational brand promise. (It should go without saying, but we'll say it anyway: You want to know what that brand promise *is* before you start creating anchors for it. Just had to get that out there.)

Five Powerful Anchors

In our world, we have defined *five* powerful, carefully chosen anchors that connect to each other, amplify each other, and support the brand promise. The first two you have already read about in this book; the third and fourth you've certainly encountered if you've had any exposure to our messaging outside of these covers. And the fifth is our motto. These five anchors are what people typically *begin conversations with* when we connect. (That's a sign that an anchor is working, by the way: People bring it up during their real-time conversations with you.)

- **Anchor #1: *The color orange.*** No surprise here. You already know that this color permeates our website, all our collateral, the company car and Kay and Steve's wardrobe choices.

- **Anchor #2: *The word and image "Moose."*** This connects, as you know, to a critical piece of our intellectual content and our brand messaging, namely the vital importance of clearly identifying your target audience. We talk about "the Moose" and "Moose bait," *all the time,* and we reference this core concept every chance we get, both visually and via our word choices. We do this for new and existing contacts alike.

- **Anchor #3:** *The phrase "Be Uncopyable."* This is our motto. It's what we are all about. It's our "Think different."

- **Anchor #4:** *The phrases "Kelly's Dad," "Marketing Gunslinger," and "Muffler Mama."* These are phrases you may not have encountered if you've never had any exposure to our messaging before picking up this book. On the other hand, if you've ever looked at Steve or Kay's LinkedIn profiles, or been on a Zoom call with Steve, or glanced at the bio that shows up on his books, *you know his daughter's name is Kelly, and Kay was the world's #1 muffler salesperson.*

- **Anchor #5:** *Stealing Genius.* This is the term we chose to call our technique for "adaptive innovation."

Those are our five primary anchors. *You should have at least three primary anchors,* but you may opt for more. Full disclosure: Getting to this point took us several years to identify and test. They didn't just land in our lap fully formed! Yours will probably take awhile to identify and test, too. That's fine. But once you have them, use them!

Big Idea #2: Make Sure at Least One Primary Anchors Optimizes Your Search Engine Results

Here's a little experiment. Type the words "Steve Miller" into your favorite search engine. You'll find that what comes up on the first page is a lot of stuff about the rock and roll guy who did (among other things) that great Eighties classic rock track "Abracadabra." Fascinating. And sure, the song's got a great beat. You can dance to it. But that page of results really doesn't get our business, or our Steve, the kind of exposure and awareness that we're looking for.

Now alter your search just a bit. Type the words "Steve Miller Uncopyable" into that same search engine. Suddenly, the online universe is all about being uncopyable!

The same happens when searching "Kay Miller, Uncopyable." But wait, there's more! Kay's nickname is "Muffler Mama." Besides the word uncopyable, it's a phrase that is unique to *her*. (It also has a special meaning, which we cover in a future chapter.) Search "Kay Miller, Muffler Mama," and you will ONLY get Kay Miller.

Do you see now how this works?

That's what happens when you make sure one of your primary anchors is a *memorable word or phrase that uniquely supports you, your brand promise, and your values.* It should also sound natural, and memorable, coming right after your name.

The anchor can come before your name, of course. For an example of this that we happen to love, do a Google search right now on the phrase "Dr. Jon Marashi, skateboarding dentist." No, he's not our client. Yes, he's just become the first and only cosmetic dentist serving famous and high-net-worth patients in Southern California that you're going to remember if the need for one ever arises in your world. (And notice that Dr. Marashi knows his Moose!)

Meet Jennie Bellinger, host of the impossible-to-forget podcast *Badass Direct Sales Mastery.* Here's what she had to say about online visibility:

> *ADHD – Attention Deficit Hyperactivity Disorder – is not just something I've been diagnosed with and talk about*

regularly. It is actually a consciously chosen aspect of my brand, and an important part of my online presence. I've always been working with direct sales problems, ever since I started the business in 2017, but the realization that my own ADHD diagnosis could be a powerful part of my brand in reaching my target audience was much more recent. It turns out that a huge number of entrepreneurs and business owners and sales professionals have ADHD, or suspect that they have it. For them, a discussion with a sales professional who has personal experience in that realm is a positive asset. Here's how I figured that out: I had a new client who was just getting started with me. When I asked her how she found me, she said she had gone to Google and typed in direct sales and ADHD. I Googled myself with those same terms and I found that I dominate the first page of Google with that combination, because I talked a lot about ADHD on my Facebook page. So ADHD is now part of the branding strategy.

But that's not all. Besides appealing to women with ADHD, Jennie does something else to attract her Moose, and completely separate her from her competition. She's created a unique brand—a brand that embraces Jennie's slightly controversial, tongue-in-cheek sense of humor.

Recently, Kay was a guest on Jennie Bellinger's podcast. Even though Kay's not in direct sales, Jennie wanted Kay's perspective on sales success, and how she earned the nickname "Muffler Mama" (explained in Chapter 7).

Kay was fascinated by Jennie's brand, and how it impacted her journey to success. She invited Jennie to be a guest on her own podcast,

"Uncopyable Women in Sales." By that point, Kay was even more intrigued, and set up a special interview with Jennie to learn more.

As you read, Jennie's Moose are women with ADHD. They're also women who are driven to succeed, and share Jennie's slightly wicked sense of humor. Jennie is known as the direct sales "Domme" (female dominant), and her branding sets her apart from every other direct sales coach. Check out her website, Badass Direct Sales Mastery (BDSM is no accident).[2] Her logo includes handcuffs and chains. She's dressed as a dominatrix, and she's holding a whip. Her branding is playful, tongue-in-cheek, and of course, a little controversial. But when she makes the promise, "I'm here to whip your business into shape," this mom of two and former middle school science teacher is dead serious.

Jennie is a certified coach who helps her clients exceed their financial goals and dream bigger dreams. She's committed to helping her clients achieve a level of financial success that supports not only themselves, but also their families. Jennie shares her own journey, including the bumps along the way, and what it took to go from failure to the top level in her direct sales business. She's extremely good at what she does, and is committed to her client's success.

Jennie embraces her unique brand, which sets herself apart from the competition in a way that's truly uncopyable.

What you're looking for here is what Jennie (and Steve and Kay!) found—a combination of words to use as anchors and result in you being the main focus when people search online for those words. This is your real estate. Claim it! Own it! Defend it!

Big Idea #3: Pick one of your five primary anchors and reference it verbally every time at the beginning of real-time interactions with your Moose.

For Steve, it's the color orange. One way or another, a reference to that color is going to happen during the first couple of minutes with a client or a prospective client. As noted, it's often the client who brings up the color orange. In the instances when the client *doesn't* reference the color orange, Steve will make a point of saying something like, "I hope you're not allergic to the color orange because if you are, I'm afraid you're not going to make it to the end of this meeting."

By the way, that line always gets a laugh. That laugh is the sound of an anchor being set. Make sure you have something equivalent to say at the beginning of your meetings!

Big Idea #4: Build your anchors into "shock and awe" mailings.

One of our favorite outreach techniques is to send a big, customized package with lots of branded collateral (all *orange*, of course!) in it to a specific Moose. We call this our Shock and Awe package.

The idea is to choose the Moose carefully enough to make the mailing make sense economically (in other words, target a high-value Moose) and to choose the collateral carefully enough to generate a "wow" response. The person on the receiving end of the package begins with deep curiosity: *Who sent this? What's it all about?* The contents of the package should convert that curiosity into "shock and awe"—as in, "Wow, they put a lot of effort into this! And they're talking about stuff that's relevant to my world! I should talk to these people!"

Let's paint you a picture of a shock and awe package we might send.

You receive an orange box (roughly 12" x 9" x 4") addressed to you. You think, *What the heck is this?* But, of course, it gets your full attention.

You open it and find a variety of items each wrapped in orange tissue paper. There is an envelope with your name on it. The note reads: "We thought you would enjoy our little goody package! Signed, Kay & Steve Miller."

As you unwrap each goody, you find: A pair of orange shoelaces, an orange umbrella, several different orange pens and pencils, orange Post-It Notes, orange rubber bands, an orange Moose whistle(!), an orange highlighter, an orange journal, an orange shotglass imprinted with a moose, autographed copies of Kay's *Uncopyable Sales Secrets* and Steve's *Uncopyable,* and two bookmarks customized for both books.

Oh yes, and a pair of orange-framed sunglasses with orange lenses.

Kay recently helped a client, CCC Washers,[3] come up with their own shock and awe package, which they sent to a very select group of prospects. They put together a package with a theme and color to fit their brand. The goal was to pique the prospect's interest and create an opportunity to have a conversation that could lead to a sale. The plan was to make follow-up calls. But as soon as their prospects started receiving the packages stuffed with goodies, CCC Washers started getting calls!

Look again at the Jim McIngvale story we shared a little earlier in this chapter, and you'll see that the package we set up for him—including Steve's book and plenty of other stuff—was a Shock and Awe mailing.

That's the power of a Shock and Awe package. It *does* get your Moose's attention.

Big Idea #5: Nurture Your Community

As we've mentioned, one of the "proof of concept" events that will tell you that you're doing all of this right is that people will *begin conversations with you by talking about one of your branding triggers.* In other words, they will turn the trigger into an anchor, in real time, during face-to-face and voice-to-voice interactions. When this happens, it is a sign that the person in question has joined your community, your tribe, if you will. (As we said before, we call our community members BFFs!) So you want to encourage and positively reinforce that behavior every time it happens. Make it a positive experience!

An example: When Kay has a guest on her podcast, she sends a thank-you note, in the mail. It's orange, of course, and includes a picture of a very important person—the guest who was on the podcast! It not only creates a fun surprise (who gets thank-you cards in the mail anymore?), it also reinforces their connection with you and your brand.

Over time as you implement the big ideas we've shared with you in this chapter, you will experience something truly remarkable, something we've learned to celebrate and treasure: Members of your community will *send you stuff in gratitude.* Posters. Original art. Greeting cards. Fan mail. Here's our advice: Celebrate it all. Acknowledge it all. Thank people personally for each and every bit of that creativity, enthusiasm, and reports from the front. Make sure each person feels heard, appreciated, and honored.

Nurture your community. Expand your BFFs and you expand your brand. Expand your brand and you expand your business. How big could it get? That's up to you.

Be sure to get your free resources at
Uncopyableyou.com/resources

NOTES

1. "Mary Kay" profile; *Forbes;* https://www.forbes.com/companies/mary-kay/?sh=1044a5802bc9; accessed November 20, 2023.

2. Follow Jennie on LinkedIn: linkedin.com/in/badassdirectsalesmastery/.

3. For more information, visit CCC Washers: https://cccwashers.com/.

7

KNOW AND PLAY TO YOUR UNIQUE STRENGTHS

Here, you learn to identify and focus with total commitment on your own **uncopyable** strengths. Just as important, you learn to delegate to others the areas where you're not so strong, so you can focus your efforts on adding the value that builds and strengthens your brand.

This chapter is all about playing to your strong suits. It's about knowing what your swing zone is and isn't.

If you are serious about leveraging your personal brand, you must get serious about the critical, potentially life-changing decision to isolate and leverage your superpower in support of that brand. Bottom line: *Figure out what you're good at that: a) adds value to others; and b) supports your brand, so you can even get better at that. In the process,*

BEING THE BEST IS GREAT, YOU'RE THE NUMBER ONE.

BEING UNIQUE IS GREATER, YOU'RE THE ONLY ONE.

—STEVE MILLER

you will notice something interesting: You'll get better and better at identifying stuff that you're not good at, so you can delegate that stuff or outsource it.

This critical personal branding strategy has a name: ***Strategic delegation.*** And you're about to get really good at it.

When the time came for us to identify someone well known who made strategic delegation the centerpiece of a successful personal branding strategy, one name quickly leaped to the top of the list. Oprah Winfrey's remarkable journey from a troubled childhood to becoming a globally recognized media mogul stands as a testament to the power of a well-crafted personal brand *and* to the power of strategic delegation.

Oprah's ability to identify her personal "superpower," strengthen it, harness it, and adeptly manage her responsibilities by entrusting others with tasks that didn't align with her strengths is, for us, the most fascinating part of her extraordinary life story. Let's look at how she developed a powerful, globally dominant personal brand by playing to her superpower and by strategically delegating responsibilities that lay beyond the borders of that superpower.

It will probably come as no surprise to learn that Oprah's superpower lies in her remarkable ability to connect with people on a profound emotional level and help them share stories that resonate universally. She recognized this unique strength early on and transformed it into the cornerstone of her emerging personal brand. As she ventured into the media landscape, Oprah realized she had a natural talent for interviewing and engaging with individuals from all walks of life. This discovery played a pivotal role in shaping her career trajectory, eventually leading to the creation of her groundbreaking talk show, "The Oprah Winfrey Show."

With laser-like focus, Oprah meticulously isolated this superpower and strategically played to it. Her exceptional interviewing skills allowed her to draw out personal stories and insights from her guests, creating an unparalleled, emotionally engaging viewing experience. Oprah's brand became synonymous with authenticity, empathy, and the capacity to delve into an astonishingly wide array of topics, ranging from entertainment to literature to pressing social issues. Her deep and honest connections with her viewers established a profound sense of trust, allowing her to address a broad spectrum of subjects.

Central to Oprah's success, however, was her willingness to delegate tasks that didn't directly align with her core strengths. Acknowledging that her brilliance lay in communication and storytelling, Oprah surrounded herself with skilled professionals who could competently manage other aspects of her business ventures. Among the tasks Oprah effectively delegated were operational, technical, and administrative responsibilities. While she remained the driving force behind her brand and content, she entrusted her business operations to experts who shared her vision.

For instance, she brought in experienced media executives and producers to handle the day-to-day management of her television shows, ensuring that the quality and impact of her programs were consistently maintained. Strategic delegation, in short, made possible every major advance in awareness of her personal brand, as well as every major expansion of the businesses she built that used that brand as their foundation. Strategic delegation is what led empowered Oprah to launch her own media production company, Harpo Productions, and later the Oprah Winfrey Network (OWN), expanding her global influence across multiple platforms.

Oprah's philanthropic endeavors also reflect both her personal brand and her commitment to strategic delegation. When it came to managing her charitable initiatives and foundations, she partnered with established organizations and professionals who specialized in social impact and community development. By doing so, she maximized her impact on causes that aligned with her values, leveraging the expertise of those who were well-versed in the intricacies of philanthropy.

One notable instance of Oprah's delegation is her partnership with Angel Network, a foundation she established to support various charitable initiatives. She collaborated with experts in various fields, allowing them to handle the logistics of organizing funds and resources for causes that resonated with her. This strategic partnership enabled her to channel her resources efficiently and effectively, leaving her free to use her unique talents to engage one-on-one with carefully chosen individuals, and spark conversations that inspire change.

Oprah Winfrey's journey showcases the immense power of a well-defined personal brand and strategic delegation. Her exceptional ability to connect with people through storytelling and empathy became the foundation of her brand's success—but leveraging that ability in the way that she has would have been impossible had she not strategically delegated operational, technical, and administrative tasks that lay beyond her swing zone.

She did not set the personal goal of becoming an expert in, say, state laws and regulations governing charitable organizations. She left that to experts she trusted, experts who shared her vision and her values. In so doing, she ensured that her brand's essence remained uncompromised while allowing others to manage the intricacies of business operations. Oprah's story stands as an inspiring example of how assessing and leveraging one's strengths, and at the same time embracing strategic delegation, can lead to a personal brand with an enduring legacy, a legacy designed to outlive its creator. That's what Oprah Winfrey has done—and from where we sit, it's not a bad aspiration.

Muffler Mama

As all the guys on the shop floor stared at her, Kay thought to herself, *So this is what it's like to install a muffler.*

Her arm strained under the weight of the welding torch above her head. Sparks showered over her Darth Vader-style helmet. A trickle of sweat ran down her back.

As a new territory manager with Walker, a leading manufacturer of automotive exhaust systems, Kay was accomplishing what she had set out to do: Learn about the product she was selling, automotive mufflers, *from the customer's perspective.* She was also leveraging her superpower: empathy.

Kay's whole career—and her personal brand—has been built on the ability to put herself in someone else's shoes, make sure that person knows firsthand she is seeing the world from their perspective, and then make a recommendation that moves the relationship forward. That's what she does for sales leaders. That's what she does for other clients. That's what she does as a consultant. It's what she's good at. It's her strong suit. Everything else, she farms out or puts at the bottom of her to-do list.

Before Kay was hired by Walker, she didn't know much about cars except how to drive one. Even that is debatable; as Steve can attest, she once backed one of the family cars into the other family car.

She learned about the Walker product line by going through the company training and studying product catalogs, brochures, and sales materials. She knew she could recite material thicknesses and statistics on engine performance and fuel economy—she had the data down cold. But she also knew that she couldn't do her job to the best of her ability yet, because she had zero experience with the product and no

WHEN YOU MAKE LOVING OTHERS THE STORY OF YOUR LIFE, THERE'S NEVER A FINAL CHAPTER, BECAUSE THE LEGACY CONTINUES. YOU LEND YOUR LIGHT TO ONE PERSON, AND HE OR SHE SHINES IT ON ANOTHER AND ANOTHER AND ANOTHER.

-OPRAH WINFREY

idea what it was like to actually install a muffler. In other words, she knew nothing of the world her prospects operated in.

Kay decided she needed to fix that. She went to Walt's Radiator and Muffler, one of her distributor's customers. She knew the manager, Wayne.

She looked Wayne in the eye and told him, "I'd like you to teach me how to install a muffler system."

Wayne looked down at the shoes Kay was wearing. Penny loafers. "Okay," he said in an amused tone. "But first, you'll need a pair of steel-toe boots."

Kay looked at his boots. The first word that came to her mind was "ugly." They were clunky, mud brown with square toes to accommodate the fact that there was actual steel underneath. She still remembers thinking of the phrase, *Your mama wears combat boots.*

Wayne sensed her reluctance. "Unless you don't mind losing a toe," he added.

Kay definitely minded.

She made an appointment with Wayne for the following week.

Later, she made her first-ever trip to Red Wing Shoes. She tried on several pairs of steel-toe boots and chose the pair she felt were the least unattractive.

The next week, she found herself clomping across the parking lot of Walt's Radiator and Muffler. Wayne looked up; no doubt he could have heard her coming a mile away. Luckily, Kay had no problem being stared at. Wayne gave her what she considered to be a respectful nod.

She followed him out to the garage, where a car was perched high on a hydraulic lift. He motioned to the car's underbelly, where Kay saw her project: An old rusted-out muffler with holes in it.

Wayne handed Kay her gear. She took the set of heavy coveralls, the thick gloves, and the aforementioned Darth Vader-style helmet. She put everything on. Wayne went to get the new muffler and the hardware Kay would need to install it. Meanwhile, a few mechanics milled around the shop, doing their best to seem nonchalant.

Kay watched while Wayne removed the old muffler. Next, he gave her a quick tutorial on using a welding torch, which was surprisingly heavy. Then she got to work. For the next 20 minutes, Wayne pointed here and there, giving Kay instructions as she attached the muffler and clamps, then welded everything to the exhaust pipes. Full disclosure: Wayne may have helped a little.

Before we go on, please allow us to provide a little context. This happened in the late 1980s. A few years earlier, a popular movie called *Flashdance* had been released. It's a feel-good movie starring Jennifer Beals, who faces obstacles in her quest to become a professional dancer. In the opening scene of the movie, the screen is very dark. We're in some sort of industrial setting. In the distance, we see sparks. And then flames. When the camera pans in, we realize the sparks and flames are coming from a person. A welder.

Suddenly the flame goes dark. The sparks stop. The welding torch is laid down. The identity of the welder, who is covered from head to toe in welding armor is still a mystery. Then slowly one arm reaches out and carefully lifts the welder's helmet. For the first time, we see the welders face. We have been assuming the welder was a man, because most welder's are. But it's not. It's a woman. Not just any woman, either. As she lifts her helmet higher, you realize it's gorgeous, sexy Jennifer Beals.

Finally, her helmet is all the way off. She gives her head a toss. The dark curls of her hair cascade down her shoulders. The camera catches her perfect face, glistening with a light glow of perspiration.

This was the picture in Kay's mind as she was welding. She kept thinking, *I'm just like Jennifer Beals in the opening scene of Flashdance!* It felt pretty cool. Eventually, they finished. The whole muffler system was installed perfectly.

Kay was ready for her Jennifer Beals moment. She put down her torch, just like Jennifer Beals. She lifted her helmet, just like Jennifer Beals. She gave her head a little toss, just like Jennifer Beals. But something didn't feel right.

As she stood there in all her Jennifer Beals wannabe glory, Kay could tell the guys in the shop were watching.

She looked at them with a smile that was probably just a little smug. Then she looked across the garage. Above the utility sink, there was a mirror.

She saw her reflection and stopped cold.

She looked like a sewer rat—a wet sewer rat.

She bore absolutely no resemblance to Jennifer Beals. That "something that didn't feel right" was her hair. Instead of cascading down her shoulders like Jennifer's, her hair was plastered flat to her head with sweat. Her face was red hot, with mascara running down both cheeks.

She looked at Wayne, embarrassed. He smiled. "Same time tomorrow?"

Okay, so she didn't look like Jennifer Beals. But learning to weld had a much bigger impact on her career than she expected. People started calling Kay "Muffler Mama." To be honest, at first she didn't love it. But then she realized what it stood for. It set her apart from her competition, and represented her story. Being Muffler Mama was real-life proof that she was willing to go the extra mile to understand, and serve, the customer. Kay didn't just observe the customer's business, she participated.

Empathy is one of Kay's superpowers. But empathy is only possible when you can put yourself in your customer's shoes—or in this case, their steel-toe boots. She's continued to live that philosophy ever since. It's become part of her brand promise: To care more about the customer than the sale. Her goal is to serve the customer's needs, no matter the outcome. That perspective is more than altruistic. It builds trust and loyalty, and leads to the outcome all sales people want—to make more sales. One of Kay's favorite compliments came from a customer who said, "Kay has become a valuable asset. I don't know what our company would do without her."

That kind of relationship takes you beyond being a "seller." You become a valued partner, someone they trust to guide them to the very best outcome, which might be a decision they hadn't even considered. They rely on your recommendation because you not only know their business, you have their best interest at heart.

If your goal is to make more sales and grow your business (and who doesn't!), start with empathy. It's the philosophy Kay lives—and the one she helps her clients create.

As for the other stuff? The list of things that don't line up with her superpower: accounting, scheduling, administrative, and all "yucks" to Kay. She either farms them out, delegates, or does them during her least productive times, when she can afford to take a breather from the major events of her day. Through it all, she never loses sight of her superpower.

And Wayne? He became one of her best customers.

Three Principles of Leverageable Superpower

Sometimes, people don't have a clear idea of what their own super-power is. Sometimes, they imagine they have a certain superpower, but they don't actually have it. Sometimes, they don't think they have *any* superpower. In our experience, everyone has *more than one* super-power they can leverage—it's just an issue of identifying the right one, confirming that it makes sense to focus your time and attention on that superpower, and then spending more and more time strengthening it, so you can deploy that superpower consistently.

The big question is not whether you *have* a superpower—trust us, you have lots of them. The big question is, how do you make sure you're strengthening the *right* superpower? After all, this is something you will be tying to the heart of your brand, something that will be at the center of everything you do. That means deciding to make a major investment of time, attention, and energy on spotlighting and amplify-ing that superpower. That's a decision you want to get right!

With that imperative in mind, consider these three guiding princi-ples we share with clients who ask us for help in determining *which* of their superpowers deserves to be built into the heart of their brand.

Principle #1: Make Sure Your Joy Overlaps with the Value You Deliver

We've talked about this before, but now seems like a good time to reinforce the point: Identifying something that you truly love doing, something that delivers substantial value to someone else—your Moose—is not just a powerful formula for personal fulfillment. It's the formula that must serve as the beating heart of your brand promise. If that heartbeat is irregular for any reason, you haven't found or leveraged the right superpower.

Passion—the unwavering motivation that is the source of all creativity—stems from doing what you genuinely love. Passion is what transforms challenges into thrilling opportunities, propelling your journey forward. Passion is what expands your expertise, which in turn gives you a better sense of what your superpower might be. Yet, when it comes to creating sustainable success in personal branding, passion on its own is not enough. Delivering value people are willing to pay for is equally crucial.

You need both passion for what you do *and* results that arise from that passion that improve the quality of someone else's life. Once you find this sweet spot, once you learn to return to it day after day after day, your superpower will likely become more evident to you. The synergy of doing what you love while delivering value can propel individuals and businesses to remarkable heights. But even when you *think* you know what the superpower is that ticks both of those boxes, it's vitally important that you seek out some kind of impartial, external validation that you are right.

Principle #2: Validate Your Superpower with a Serious Self-Assessment

Full disclosure: Some of this you can do on your own, and some you'll need a little help with. Yes, even though the self-assessment is your project, your journey, and your responsibility, a truly comprehensive self-assessment is eventually going to involve working with a team, or a resource, that doesn't know you personally so you can get a clearer sense of both your strong suits and your blind spots.

But we're getting ahead of ourselves. Let's look first at nine things you can do, and should do, without the input of any outside system. Think of these as journal entry assignments and get ready to spend some time writing. In our experience, it's best to set aside at least a day for this kind of journal work.

On Your Own, Do Some Detailed Journaling

1. Spotlight Your Technical Skills: Break down your technical skills into specific areas. For example, if you're in the field of digital marketing, list skills like SEO, social media management, content creation, and data analysis. Rate your proficiency in each skill on a scale of 1 to 10.

2. Spotlight Your Soft Skills: Explore your soft skills, which are equally important. These might include communication, leadership, adaptability, problem-solving, and creativity. Reflect on instances where you've demonstrated these skills effectively.

3. Spotlight Your Certifications and Qualifications: List any certifications or qualifications you hold. These formal credentials can validate your skills and expertise for people who are unfamiliar with your work. These may or may not relate to your personal brand, but you should get them down in black and white.

4. Spotlight Your Transferable Skills: Consider skills that can be applied across various industries, such as project management, teamwork, or time management. These skills are versatile and often sought after.

5. Quantify Your Achievements: What are you proudest of accomplishing in your career thus far? Make a list. Make it a long one. Spend some time on this. As you list your notable achievements, be sure to quantify them whenever possible. For instance, instead of writing "increased sales," specify by how much they increased: "Increased sales by 30 percent in six months."

6. *Quantify Your Impact:* Describe how your achievements positively impacted *any* business or organization. Did they lead to cost savings, revenue growth, improved customer satisfaction, or enhanced efficiency?

7. *Identify the Biggest Challenges You've Overcome:* Highlight the challenges or obstacles you faced when accomplishing these achievements. This demonstrates your problem-solving skills and your resilience.

8. *List the Recognitions and Awards:* If you received any recognition, awards, or accolades for your accomplishments, include them. They add credibility to your achievements.

9. *Track the Long-Term Impact:* Write about the lasting impact of your achievements. Did they pave the way for further successes or innovations in your field? Did they point you or anyone toward a new market? Toward innovations that made a difference?

Appeal to an Outside System

Journaling as we've just laid out for you will doubtless give you some insight into where your superpowers lie and what value they deliver. But your self-assessment isn't complete until you work with a resource, team, or system that *isn't* personally associated with you and can give you a detailed, authoritative breakdown of where your capacities and your blind spots are showing up.

One good resource we've used ourselves, and have recommended to clients, is 16Personalities.com, a proven assessment tool that gives you detailed information about what really drives, inspires, worries, and demotivates you, so you can get a better idea of what you do well, what you're better off delegating to others if you possibly can, and what you should avoid entirely.

Not only that, this resource gives you some great tools for interacting effectively with the other 15 personality types! This site has the twin advantages of being reliable, tested in multiple environments, and free—so there's really no excuse not to at least see what it has to offer. The website promises a "freakishly accurate" description of who you are and why you do things the way you do. In our experience, the company lives up to that brand promise.

Another great resource—involving a more significant investment of time and resources—is available at jocrf.org, home of the Johnson O'Connor Research Foundation, which offers a comprehensive two-day in-person assessment of aptitudes and natural talents, some of which you may not even have realized you had. It's a major undertaking, granted, but the results are so strikingly detailed, and so accurate, that we felt we had to recommend them in this part of the book.

The JOCRF website explains: "Just like scientists use data to make predictions, aptitude testing can help you predict the types of careers you'll thrive in. Our work is rooted in the scientific study of human abilities and the mission of our founder, Johnson O'Connor, who believed that everyone has natural talents that should be nurtured and used." If you're really serious about self-assessment—and in our view, you should be—you will, at some point, want to consider booking a session with Johnson O'Connor. This assessment will clearly and definitively identify, not just what you're good at and what you're not so good at, but *what you do better than most other people.* If that's not relevant to your brand and your brand promise, we don't know what is!

A side note: Steve invested in this assessment at the age of 32, when it became clear to him that his dream of becoming a professional golfer was not going to pan out. He decided he needed to do a deep dive, which is precisely what Johnson O'Connor delivered. Among (many) other things, the assessment told Steve that he was not likely to be a good surgeon or a good airplane pilot, but that he *was* likely to be a highly successful teacher, speaker, and trainer. Steve opted to play to his strengths as the assessment had identified them, and the rest, as they say, is history.

Principle #3: Validate Your Superpower by Getting Others' Objective Feedback

Once you complete the first two steps, you should have a pretty good sense of what a superpower that supports your brand promise is. Now the question is: Do the people who know you best agree with you?

Reaching out to friends, colleagues, and trusted individuals for their insights on whether you are on the right track about: a) What your superpower is; and b) whether it delivers value worth paying for is absolutely essential. Consider this step non-negotiable! Pick people who will tell you the truth, and then ask them directly whether you are genuinely excelling in what you're passionate about and whether your work is delivering tangible value.

You might want to consider giving them a brief questionnaire to fill out, which you can then ask them to expand on in informal conversation. This kind of input is invaluable because it acts as a reality check, ensuring that your self-assessment aligns with external perceptions. It helps you avoid the trap of self-delusion, where enthusiasm might cloud your ability to accurately gauge your impact.

Constructive feedback can also highlight blind spots and areas for improvement, which may end up making your superpower even more potent or, who knows, helping you to identify an entirely different superpower, one you had previously overlooked! (Remember, you have more than one.)

Ask questions. Evaluate and accept the feedback. Adjust accordingly. When others you trust confirm that your passion and value delivery are in full alignment, their validation of your results means you can solidify your brand's promise by moving forward with full commitment. That validation means your target audience—your Moose—is more likely to engage with, support, and pay for something they perceive as genuinely valuable and authentic. And it means you're more likely to be able to build and expand a *community* rooted in your brand promise.

Be sure to get your free resources at
Uncopyableyou.com/resources

8

FIND AND LEVERAGE YOUR PERSONAL BRANDING MESSAGE

Master the art of getting your voice heard.

In the realm of personal branding, the term "platform strategy" refers to a deliberate and structured approach to establishing and promoting oneself across various mediums or channels. It involves identifying the most effective platforms, such as social media, blogs, podcasts, or public speaking engagements, that align with your message, your values, and your target audience—your Moose.

A well-executed platform strategy enables you to showcase your expertise, share your unique perspective, and connect with your audience in a consistent and engaging manner. It also involves considering how to leverage each platform's strengths and audience demographics to maximize your reach and impact.

The key to a successful platform strategy lies in two concerns: *Authenticity* and *providing value to your audience.* Your strategy must be an extension of your brand promise and a means to foster genuine connections with those who resonate with your work. One man in particular showcased a personal mastery of these often overlooked, often neglected concerns—and he did so long before platforms like blogs and podcasts even existed.

The Platform Strategist Who Started It All

Mark Twain (the *brand*, created in 1863) was created by Samuel Langhorne Clemens (the man, born in 1835). Over a long period of years, Clemens, a hard-working river pilot-turned-writer, built up the Twain persona—a blend of wit, irreverence, and keen, thought-provoking social commentary. In the process, he seems to have merged with his own personal brand, creating not just a stream of American literary classics including *The Adventures of Tom Sawyer* and *The Adventures of Huckleberry Finn,* but also a public role that Clemens excelled in playing: The public version of the author of those books. Twain, or was it Clemens?

Thus he emerged not only as one of the literary giants of the nineteenth century (he's been called the "father of American literature"), but as a brand statement himself, and as a true pioneer in the realm of platform-driven personal branding. Sometimes it was, and is, difficult to identify the border between Clemens and Twain. For the sake of convenience, we'll refer to this groundbreaking figure by the name most people use when referring to him: Mark Twain.

Twain's strategic approach to maximizing engagement with his target audience revolutionized the way writers connected with their readers, leaving a lasting impact on the worlds of literature and marketing alike. Today, we would call what Twain accomplished in the three extraordinary decades of his career that unfolded after 1880— *effective platform strategy in support of a powerful personal brand.* Back then, however, there simply was no word or phrase for what the man was doing. Like a lot of innovators, he opted to change the rules of the game in which he chose to play—to disrupt his industry and build a new one it its place. Twain himself, it turned out, *was* that industry.

Here's the point. The innovations Mark Twain's disruptions brought to the emerging disciplines of publishing, public relations, and branding still stand, a century and a half later, as powerful, practical examples of the all-important art of finding and leveraging the right platforms for broadcasting the right message. He was, in short, a master at getting his voice heard. Let's look briefly at how he did that.

In 1884, Twain, already one of the most famous men in America and the dominant brand in American book publishing (his first channel), became a pioneer in the previously under-explored realm of paid speaking events (his second channel). Recognizing the immense potential of public speaking as a source of both visibility and income, he embarked on a series of highly successful lecture tours in the United States and abroad.

Twain recognized, and leveraged, the power of direct, in-person engagement with his audience, regaling paying audiences with a steady stream of humorous anecdotes and keen observations. His strong vocal skills and engaging, witty delivery made him a popular speaker, and he used these tours to entertain and to promote his written works. His use of speaking engagements to support personal visibility, book sales, and income from speaking itself was innovative in the US at the time. Charles Dickens had developed the idea in Great Britain; Dickens and Twain paved the way for countless authors and public figures who would follow in their footsteps.

Twain sold out speaking halls and captivated listeners, solidifying his reputation as a literary luminary, and instantly dominating a (literal!) platform for self-promotion and messaging that he had built from scratch. As a result of these wildly successful speaking engagements, Twain created what might today be termed a "rock star" persona, long before the concept of "rock star" existed.

Another platform he dominated consciously and strategically in support of his personal brand was print media. Especially in his later years, Twain's talent for getting and sustaining attention from journalists was simply unparalleled, because it was endlessly innovative. He never stopped coming up with new ideas for winning coverage.

You may or may not be aware that Twain's brand was, in the final decade of his life, strongly anchored in a specific visual cue: His now-famous white suit. This anchoring was a conscious choice, one that Twain knew would enhance his visibility, not just among the everyday readers he wanted to reach, but also among the reporters, editors, and cultural figures of his day. These were the people who shaped public opinion about what did and didn't constitute writing worth reading.

Today we would call the tastemakers Twain was trying to reach "members of the mainstream media" and "influencers." We would call the newspapers and magazines they wrote for "platforms." Twain was very, very good at communicating through those platforms. And one of the most effective ways he found for doing that was wearing a suit (to use his words) "made out of linen so white it hurt your eyes to look at it."

Many of the people who saw that suit, Twain knew, would be reporters looking for something interesting to write about—reporters who worked for newspapers that would help determine what readers would and would not be talking about the following day. He knew that reporters—and indeed all human beings—tend to talk about and write about what stands out, what they find memorable, what they can't help noticing. So, why not *dress* in something people can't help noticing? This was a breakthrough idea for optimizing the platform of newspapers, magazines, and journals. And it worked.

Twain first put this game-changing idea into practice shortly before he showed up to testify at a Congressional hearing on copyright legislation. He used the opportunity to deliver on his personal brand promise: The promise to *entertain readers.* He did that by attracting attention, then creating and delivering what might today be called "sound bites"—but what in the late nineteenth century were still known as "quotes." And when it came to attracting attention and being quotable—his platform strategy of choice when he knew editors and reporters were present—Twain had no serious competition.

While waiting to testify before Congress, Twain shared some of his carefully prepared "spontaneous" remarks with reporters. "Why don't you ask why I am wearing such apparently unseasonable clothes?" he said. Then without waiting for anyone to answer the question, Twain continued:

> *I'll tell you. I have found that when a man reaches the advanced age of seventy-one years, as I have, the continual sight of dark clothing is likely to have a depressing effect upon him. Light-colored clothing is more pleasing to the eye and enlivens the spirit. Now, of course, I cannot compel everyone to wear such clothing just for my especial benefit, so I do the next best thing and wear it myself.*
>
> *Of course, before a man reaches my years the fear of criticism might prevent him from indulging his fancy. I am not*

afraid of that. I am decidedly for pleasing color combinations in dress. I like to see the women's clothes, say, at the opera. What can be more depressing than the sombre black which custom requires men to wear upon state occasions? A group of men in evening clothes looks like a flock of crows, and is just about as inspiring. After all, what is the purpose of clothing? Are not clothes intended primarily to preserve dignity and also to afford comfort to their wearer? Now I know of nothing more uncomfortable than the present-day clothes of men. The finest clothing made is a person's own skin, but, of course, society demands something more than this.

Reporters took it all down verbatim; their editors loved it. Twain's remarks garnered wide circulation, and his appearance was a sensation. The next day, Twain's suit—not Congress's ongoing debate over the minute details of copyright legislation—was the story the whole country couldn't seem to stop talking about. Here's how the *Washington Post* covered the event, in a story entitled "Twain's Fancy Suit": "In spite of the keen December wind blowing outside, he burst into view, garbed in a cream-colored suit of light summer flannel. The effect was decidedly startling; it fairly made one shiver to look at him."

That dazzling white suit became Twain's trademark. For a long time, he did not appear in public in any other attire. And everywhere Twain wore white, people seemed to talk about him more and write about him more. The white suit became and remains to this day, a central element, not just of Twain's brand, but of his relentless effort to connect with his audience personally, using communication platforms he knew they favored.

Your efforts must be similarly relentless and similarly innovative.

For Example...

Steve's friend Dan Thurmon is a prolific writer and inspirational speaker widely celebrated for his dynamic approach to performance and athletics. Dan delivers powerful, transformative insights on life mastery along three parallel lines: Mind, body, and spirit.

Dan is what we would call a luminary thought leader. And he's the only thought leader we know who's also an acrobat. After completing his studies at the University of Georgia, where he pursued a degree in business, he embarked on a journey that would merge his passion for athletics and the stage with his dedication to self-improvement. He became a prolific writer, penning insightful, popular works on peak performance, personal growth, and achieving true potential. Dan's books show readers how to transcend self-imposed limitations and lead more fulfilling lives. If we could only point you toward one of them, it would be *Positive Chaos: Transform Crisis into Clarity and Advantage*. Read that after you've finished this book. You'll be glad you did.

Anyway. Dan seamlessly integrated his background in theater arts, acrobatics, and improvisation with some truly groundbreaking insights on human performance. This fusion created a unique in-person experience that, for years, resonated deeply with audiences worldwide.

And then Covid changed everything.

Which meant Dan's platform strategy had to change, too.

During a recent interview, Dan told us, "I was used to giving keynote programs, and of course I wasn't alone in that. But the shift away from live meetings hit me particularly hard because live meetings were kind of central to what I did. Before the pandemic, leading a keynote event meant one thing: Getting on an airplane and going where the client wanted me to go, so I could present my message to them, in person. And that in-person connection meant a lot to me because of my personal focus on performance and interaction with a live audience. But when Covid hit, we had to make some changes. Those changes began with the task of re-imagining what a keynote speech could be." He continued:

> So that's what we got to work on. Now the types of experiences that people have when I deliver my talks fall into three categories: mind, body and spirit. And of course, there's a physicality to what I had done up to that point to deliver each of those experiences. I used my physical sense of self to teach what I teach, because physicality is just the essence of who I am.
>
> It's very important that there's a physicality in my message because that's one way I get people thinking differently. So we touch all three: mind, the headspace, the physical body, and then the spiritual connection, which can also be understood as personal growth. Because I believe, why even bother doing this if we're not touching people at the soul level, and helping them grow and see things in new ways? And my physical presence and my ability to engage with an audience in person was really central to all of that. But when Covid hit, I decided we had to pivot. I had to translate what I was doing in person to a virtual environment. So the challenge was, Well, how do I do this in the studio?
>
> I got some help on answering that question, and the end result was three different sets, each custom-designed, and each of which could be used for remote delivery of my keynote presentations. There's one set for mind, one set for body,

and one set for spirit. And the three environments each present a unique visual engagement with a remote viewer. They've basically become a new kind of performance art for us, a new kind of digital keynote delivery—a whole new platform. And it's proved so popular that we've kept it going, even after the pandemic receded.

In other words, Dan did exactly what Mark Twain did. He found out where and how his target audience wanted to engage. And he designed and used a customized platform strategy that was authentic to him—and he reached that audience.

1. Identify and Leverage Suitable Platforms

- Evaluate various platforms (social media, blogs, podcasts, public speaking, etc.) to determine which ones align with your message, values, and target audience.

- Take inspiration from Mark Twain and Dan Thurmon on how they utilized different platforms, like public speaking and digital delivery respectively, to engage with their audience.

2. Innovate and Adapt

- Be open to pivoting your strategy or exploring new platforms to continue effectively engaging with your audience, especially during changing circumstances, similar to how Dan Thurmon adapted his approach during the Covid pandemic.

- Consider creating memorable, distinguishing aspects of your brand (like Mark Twain's white suit) that capture attention and enhance visibility across chosen platforms.

3. Maximize Platform Strengths

- Investigate the unique strengths and audience demographics of each platform to optimize your reach and impact. For example, if a platform has a younger demographic and supports video content, tailor your message to resonate with that audience using engaging video presentations.

- Similarly, analyze the analytics provided by these platforms to understand what content performs well and why, and use this insight to refine your strategy.

4. Experiment with Visual and Interactive Elements

- Incorporate visual cues or interactive elements to create a memorable brand identity and engage your audience in a meaningful way. Like Mark Twain's white suit and our color orange branding, having a visual cue could make you more recognizable and memorable to your audience.

- If applicable, explore interactive engagements like Q&A sessions, webinars, or live events to foster a direct connection with your audience. This could also be a space to receive real-time feedback, which can be invaluable for adjusting your strategy and understanding your audience's preferences and responses to your brand and message.

Be sure to get your free resources at
Uncopyableyou.com/resources

9

SEIZE OPPORTUNITIES TO GROW FROM SETBACKS

Learn to identify value, potential, and branding inspiration in every obstacle you encounter—as you master and perfect the non-negotiable delivery of your message to your target audience in a resonating way.

In the annals of history, few figures have emerged from horror and tragedy with the tenacity and fortitude exhibited by Malala Yousafzai—and none serve as a better example of effective, authentic personal branding in the twenty-first century.

Malala's extraordinary journey from a young Pakistani girl facing the horrors of Taliban oppression to an international symbol of hope, resilience, and education, is a testament to the transformative power of a mission that connects powerfully to a legitimate personal brand, a personal brand rooted in strong personal belief.

Malala, the world's youngest Nobel Prize winner, has crafted a powerful global brand centered on the fundamental right to education for every girl. Let's unravel the alchemical process by which Malala turned adversity into advocacy, casting a light on her profound impact on the world.

Malala's story begins in the Swat Valley of Pakistan. Born in 1997, she grew up in an environment where the simple act of attending school was, for girls, an act of defiance. She committed that act, with the support of her family, and spoke out forcefully to anyone who would listen to her about the non-negotiable reality that education is a basic human right for all of us, including young girls. The turning point came in 2012, when a Taliban gunman boarded her school bus and shot her in the head. This unspeakable act was meant to silence her. It failed.

Despite grave injury, the 15-year-old was flown to a Pakistani military hospital, then to an intensive care unit in England. After a week and a half in a coma, Yousafzai awoke up in an English hospital bed. She had survived the attack. Following a difficult recovery, she recommitted herself to her mission and sought a global platform that would enable her to talk, not just to Pakistan, but to all of humanity, about her mission: A world where education for girls is as automatic and unquestioned as education for boys.

Malala's survival, her advocacy, and her willingness to continue to speak out against violence and religious extremism at great personal risk became a beacon of hope for millions. The world watched in awe as she emerged from a potentially debilitating injury and spoke her truth, louder and louder on a global stage, her voice now imbued with a moral power that religious extremists simply could not match,

Malala's journey from victim to global advocate was not solely a result of circumstance. It was a choice, a deliberate, strategic exercise in personal branding. With the unwavering support of her family, she harnessed the power of storytelling, utilizing her personal experiences as a powerful brand narrative, and as a catalyst for social change. Her memoir, *I Am Malala,* became a cornerstone of her brand, providing readers with a poignant and intimate glimpse into her life, her struggles, and her unyielding commitment to education. By 2017, the book had sold more than two million copies.

Furthermore, Malala's magnetic presence on the global stage, characterized by her eloquence and unwavering conviction, solidified her as a symbol of hope for millions. Her speeches at the United Nations and other international forums resonated with audiences worldwide, transcending borders and cultural divides. Through her words, she spoke not only for herself but for the countless girls whose voices had been silenced.

She won the Nobel Peace Prize at just 17 years of age.

Examples of Malala's expertise in personal branding are evident in the following:

1. Media Savvy and Authenticity: Malala's interactions with the media exemplify her mastery of personal branding. Her interviews and public appearances radiate genuineness, allowing audiences to connect with her on a deeply personal level about her experiences and deeply held beliefs. Whether speaking with world leaders or sharing moments of vulnerability with a television interviewer, Malala remains true to herself, reinforcing the sincerity of her mission.

2. Strategic Partnerships: Beyond her individual efforts, Malala has strategically aligned herself with influential figures and organizations that share her commitment to education. Collaborations with renowned activists, philanthropists, and educators have amplified her message and expanded her reach, demonstrating a keen understanding of how partnerships can enhance her brand's impact.

3. Digital Presence and Social Media Influence: Malala's adept use of digital platforms has further solidified her brand. Her presence on social media channels provides a direct line of communication with her global audience. Through compelling storytelling, thought-provoking posts, and timely updates, she maintains an engaged community of supporters, leveraging the power of technology to advance her cause.

4. Mission Focus. Central to Malala's brand is her unequivocal commitment to her personal mission: To ensure that every girl has access to quality education. This clarity of purpose has been the North Star guiding her advocacy efforts. Through the establishment of the Malala Fund, she has mobilized resources and partnered with organizations worldwide to further this cause. By leveraging her brand, she has opened doors and garnered support from individuals, corporations, and governments, all united by a shared belief in the transformative power of education.

Malala Yousafzai's journey from a young girl in the Swat Valley with strong beliefs to a global icon of education advocacy is a testament to the remarkable alchemy of which the human spirit is capable, when it expresses honest beliefs. Her ability to transmute personal tragedy into a powerful global brand is a master class in resilience, determination, and purpose-driven activism. She has not just overcome unspeakable adversity, she has built her experiences and insights in dealing with that adversity—and her active use of those experiences to effect positive change, into a personal brand like no other.

A Special Chapter

This Chapter 9 of the book is all about taking the direct, first-person experience of adversity and finding a way to alchemize that experience into opportunity, into a deeper personal sense of purpose, and ultimately into a successful branding effort. It is a special chapter—a chapter that means a lot to us for three reasons.

The first reason this is special is that *the act of redefining, repurposing, and rechanneling instances of opposition, tragedy, and suffering can—if you are honest with yourself and authentic to your values—present you with some truly remarkable brand narratives* you can share with the world. Malala's story is certainly an example of this.

Another good example comes from W Mitchell, a well-known motivational speaker, businessman, and member of the International Speakers Hall of Fame. Years ago, he was burned over 65 percent of his body when a truck made an unexpected turn in front of his motorcycle. He recovered, but his face and hands were deeply scarred and most of his ten fingers were gone.

Somehow, he bounced back from this devastating event. Just a few years later, he had co-founded a successful company that made highly energy-efficient wood-burning stoves. While undertaking a business trip on behalf his company, the small aircraft he was piloting one bitterly cold morning crashed on takeoff, because of ice that had built up on the plane's wings. The other passengers on the plane walked away; he did not. His spinal cord was injured, and he was now paralyzed for life from the waist down.

Those are two instances of physical suffering and trauma that most people would have a hard time imagining bouncing back from. But bounce back W Mitchell did, running for, and winning, election to the office of mayor of Crested Butte, Colorado, from a wheelchair. W is a friend of ours, and he has emerged as an inspiration to millions of people around the world who see, in his personal story, a powerful lesson—adversity does not define anyone. He shares, "I'm not going to dwell on the four thousand or so things I can't do. I'm only going to focus on the six thousand things I *can* do."

The second reason this chapter is special is that it connects to *the vitally important topic of personal character.* How you handle the major adversity that arises in your life—and most of us eventually *do* encounter some major adversity—defines you as a person. Even if you decide *not* to build your personal experience with adversity into your personal branding campaign, and plenty of successful people choose *not* to share that kind of story publicly, your choice of response to the challenges that come your way will always be extremely for your business, and for you as a person. In this chapter, we aim to show you that setbacks, whether they become part of your brand narrative or not, show up in your life for a reason—to open your eyes to what you are truly capable of.

And the third reason this chapter is special is that it presents *us* with a special kind of challenge as the authors of this book. Why? Because we know that anytime someone examines the problem of identifying purpose, meaning, and forward momentum in events that are tragic or painful, that person is also, whether they admit it or not, examining the topic of *personal spirituality.* Some people don't like acknowledging this directly. They talk around the subject, because they've been told that spirituality is a topic that doesn't belong in a business book. We disagree. We believe *religion*—that is, proselytizing—has no place in a business book. But we also believe a practical, purpose-driven approach to big questions, an approach that acknowledges the influence and calling of a higher power, makes it much, much easier for you to make sense of, and integrate, the painful events of your life. Once you integrate them, you can learn from them, move on, and make a contribution, via your business and your personal branding on behalf of that business.

So the challenge we have set for ourselves in this chapter is to show you how your unique sense of purpose, your own sense of your life's journey, your deepening sense of who you are and why you're here, can connect to the personal experience of adversity and create meaning for you as an individual. You'll have to be the judge of whether we succeed in that effort. But we're going to try. And we're going to start with something Steve experienced directly as a child.

Steve's Experience

(Note: the rest of this chapter is in Steve's voice and from his perspective. You'll understand why as you go along.)

As a young child, only 12 years old, I was diagnosed with a form of muscular dystrophy called myasthenia gravis. It's a genetic condition that can gradually cause human muscles to weaken more rapidly than they should. It's sometimes very serious, leading to severe disability and death, and there's no known cure.

Early on it wasn't a huge deal. I was still pretty active, just slowing down a bit. I would tire easily. As I grew older, maybe 14-15 years old, sports became difficult. My doctor started me on medication, pyrodostigmine (Mestinon). It didn't make things all better, and he explained that on a good day, it might get me to about 70 percent of a normal person's strength, stamina, and endurance.

I think the thing that really woke me up to my situation were some pamphlets my doctor sent. One in particular "educated" me on the type of girl I should look for as I grew up. It warned me to look for someone who wasn't super active, especially not into highly active sports. "Look for someone who is happy to stay at home and read or watch TV," I remember reading, "Don't look for someone who wants to go dancing."

I remember thinking, *But what if I want to go dancing?* I really started to understand the seriousness of my situation.

For years, I've hesitated to mention in my speeches that I was ever diagnosed with myasthenia gravis. I've steered clear because something like this is intensely personal and I didn't want people to feel sorry for me. I was also sensitive to others who might have something like myasthenia gravis today and not be able to do what I did.

You see, I ultimately walked away from it. I'm totally fine and haven't taken any drugs for it in 45 years.

I feel a little more comfortable mentioning now, in my later years, that, as a young child, after I was diagnosed, something happened to me. You can call it a dream. You can call it a vision. I don't really know what to call it. All I can tell you was that, in the middle of the night, I heard someone talking to me. I clearly heard a man's voice say to me, "Steve, what if your 70 percent was equal to a normal person's 100 percent?"

In other words, like W Mitchell's perspective, I was being told to focus on what I could do, what I could accomplish, not what I couldn't. It was at that point that I committed to build myself up, body, mind, and soul—to raise the level to where I could do anything I wanted to do. So that was kind of a turning point for me, the point at which I decided to raise myself up, physically and in terms of my personal belief system. Well, as it turned out, when I did that, I was able to just basically walk away from the disease.

And now, decades later, I'm handed another diagnosis: Parkinson's. And the minute I heard that from the doctor, something inside my head just clicked. A little voice inside said, *You know how to handle this.* And I do. I'm focusing on what I can do. Not on what I can't.

This chapter is all about turning apparent adversity into advantage in your personal branding campaign. That subject is a subset of a much larger, much more consequential subject, namely, turning apparent adversity into advantage in your life.

Here's one of my favorite teaching stories that connects to that lesson. It comes from the Buddhist tradition.

A farmer and his son had a cherished stallion who helped them scratch a meager living from their humble farm. One day, the horse wandered off. After five days of searching, the horse was nowhere to be found. The farmer and the son accepted that they had lost their prize stallion. Their neighbors exclaimed, "Your horse has strayed, what an unfortunate turn!" The farmer responded, "Perhaps, perhaps not. We will see."

After a few days, however, the horse returned home, accompanied by a few wild mares. The neighbors cheered, "Your horse has returned, and brought several horses with it. What great fortune!" The farmer calmly said, "Perhaps, perhaps not. We will see."

Later that week, the farmer's son attempted to tame one of the mares. She threw him to the ground, and the boy broke his leg. The villagers lamented, "Your son has a broken leg now, and you must do most of the work on the farm without his help. What a terrible stroke of misfortune!" The farmer replied, "Perhaps, perhaps not. We will see."

A few weeks passed, and soldiers from the national army marched through town, conscripting all able-bodied boys for service. They did not, however, take the farmer's son, as he was still recuperating from his injury. Friends exclaimed, "Your boy has been spared, what incredible luck!" To which the farmer serenely remarked, "Perhaps, perhaps not. We will see."

I love that story because it really drives the point home: "Good" and "bad," "fortunate," and "unfortunate" are not realities in and of themselves. They're labels that human beings attach to their experience. If we buy into them as though they were the final word on our experience, or let others apply them to what we encounter in life, we're skewing our perspective, often in directions that aren't particularly helpful.

Consider my situation. The myasthenia gravis story I shared with you doesn't define me, and the experience I had with myasthenia gravis wasn't good or bad in and of itself. It just happened. It was one of those events that shows up in life. I can't say that it was fundamentally good or bad, lucky or unlucky. What I can say, though, is that the older I get, the more obvious it becomes to me that apparent adversity has always given me something that I needed to learn.

Seen from this perspective, I can see that adversity has been a curious, predictable catalyst in the forward trajectory of my career, my relationships, and my own sense of purpose. That early experience with myasthenia gravis, for instance, has provided me with some fascinating turning points. Right now I want to share a couple of those turning points with you, so that you can be better positioned to have your own "We'll see" moment the next time something that looks really, really bad (or for that matter, really really good) happens in your life. Who knows what it really means, or what it has to do with your brand? Time will tell. We'll see.

I've already told you about the first of those turning points: That dream, or vision, or whatever it was, that inspired me to focus on what was possible, as opposed to what was not possible, in my life. That dream, vision, or whatever it was has helped me immeasurably in the years since. Not only that, it led me to the second big turning point, which has to do with a remarkable gentleman by the name of Robert H. Schuller.

The Crystal Cathedral Changes Everything

The late Reverend Robert H. Schuller was a friend of mine. Schuller was one of the most prominent American televangelists, known for his positive and highly motivational preaching style in the vein of Dr. Norman Vincent Peale, his friend and mentor. Schuller was also a bestselling author of practical, results-focused books about positive thinking, such as *Tough Times Never Last, But Tough People Do*. He touched millions of people with his pragmatic, accessible messages of personal empowerment and spiritual renewal.

All the way back in 1994, Dr. Schuller invited me to appear as a guest on his Hour of Power television program, which at that point was one of the most widely viewed weekly religious broadcasts in the world with over twelve million viewers. In the beautiful Crystal Cathedral, he interviewed me about my experiences with myasthenia gravis. Schuller must have liked what I had to say, because he kind of took me under his wing.

After the broadcast, he and I were out having brunch, and we were really connecting, really having a great conversation. I remember at one point he looked at me and said, "You know, Steve, you were pretty comfortable up there in front of an audience of a couple of thousand people. You did a really good job. You might want to consider becoming a professional speaker."

"A professional speaker?" I said. "You mean, people get paid for just speaking?" I had no idea at that point that there was an entire industry built around professional speaking, that there was a huge professional association, the National Speakers Association, devoted to it, or that people like Zig Ziglar, and Cavett Robert had built considerable commercial empires around their speaking engagements.

"Oh, yeah," Dr. Schuller said. "You can get paid very, very well if you're good enough. And I think you could be quite good at this."

So we got into this whole conversation about what that kind of career would look like. Eventually I asked him, "Well, how do you find people who are willing to pay a lot of money to have someone come and speak at their event?"

That turned out to be a fateful question for me, because the answer Schuller gave me ended up shaping my entire professional career—and the advice I would pass along to countless clients as a consultant.

"Let me answer that question by posing another one," Dr. Schuller said. "How do you hunt moose?"

It was (and still is, for someone unprepared for it) a bizarre question. What was he talking about? "Moose?" I said. "You want to know how I hunt moose?"

"Right," Dr. Schuller said, smiling. "Would you go to Florida to hunt moose?"

I thought for a second or two, then said, "No, I guess I would go to…I don't know, Canada or maybe Alaska or Maine or New Hampshire if I wanted to hunt moose."

"Correct," Dr. Schuller said. "You have to go to where the moose are hanging out. Right?"

And I said, "Okay." I was starting to see where he was going with this.

Then he said, "Well, what would you use to attract them? I mean, would you set out Hostess Ding Dongs or Twinkies or candy bars, and expect them to show up in large numbers?"

I thought for a moment, then said, "No, no, I guess I'd have to find some kind of moose bait."

"Exactly right," Dr. Schuller replied. "And once you're face to face with a moose, you're not going to bring it down with a tennis racket, are you?"

And I said, "No, I'm going to need to get myself a moose gun."

"Right," he said.

So after he shared that little metaphor with me—which perhaps you've noticed now serves as one of the foundation blocks of my consulting business—he said, "Look, I think you should think about doing this professionally. I want to introduce you to some friends of mine who are successful professional speakers. And then you can see if this speaking thing is right for you. Does that make sense?"

Now at that point, I was working as the VP of Sales and Marketing for a Japanese toy company. This sounded much, much more exciting. So I said yes.

That discussion launched my career. Schuller opened my eyes to a completely different way of making a life for myself, a life that was all about making a difference in other people's lives. I started speaking, and what I got paid for speaking about was marketing and, eventually, branding. That led directly to the business Kay and I now run together.

Why do I tell you all of this? Well, think about this from the point of view of someone being dealt what looks, at first glance, like a bad hand. Think about it from the point of view of someone being told, as a child, that he has a form of muscular dystrophy. And part of that kid thinks, *This is it. This is the worst thing that has ever happened.* But eventually, another part of that kid, a voice from deep inside, says, "Perhaps, perhaps not. We will see."

If I had never been diagnosed with myasthenia gravis, I would certainly have never been on the Hour of Power. If I had never been on the Hour of Power, I would never have had that conversation with Dr. Schuller. And if I had never had that conversation with him, I wouldn't be doing, and loving, what I am doing now!

There is a path for you. Don't prejudge it. Walk it. See what happens. Keep an open mind. Keep moving forward. See what you learn along the way. See what you can use. And when you come up against a challenge, and part of you is convinced something terrible has happened to you, do yourself a favor. Set a clear limit to the amount of time you *choose* to spend being mad or sad or victimized by what's happened: Fifteen minutes, one hour, maybe as long as one day, depending on the situation. But once that time is up—move on.

And once you do move on, never, ever stop repeating that mantra I've shared with you, the mantra that fits neatly into any and every belief system: "We will see."

Be sure to get your free resources at Uncopyableyou.com/resources

10

FINALIZE YOUR BATTLE PLAN AND EXECUTE IT!

In this final chapter, you will pull together everything you've learned about personal branding. You'll design and begin to execute your personal battle plan. You will also receive some important guidance from us on how to monitor your progress toward important goals. And you'll learn how to figure out when it's time to change tactics in response to changing circumstances—without changing your vision or your values.

It's time for you to act on what you've learned in this book by creating your own unique personal branding plan and then implementing that plan. This book's Big Idea is cited again, followed by a concise overview of the key Uncopyable Personal Branding Best Practices we've shared with you earlier in the book. Each of those Uncopyable Personal Branding Best Practices is followed by a series of questions.

Our challenge to you in this final chapter is a simple one: Come up with an answer, in your own words, at length, and based on your own situation, to each of those questions. We recommend you write down your best answers on a few sheets of paper, and then post those sheets someplace you will see them each day. This will make it easier for you to execute the plan.

THE BIG IDEA

Create a personal brand that gets people to know you, like you, trust you, and **remember** you!

UNCOPYABLE personal branding empowers you to create your own rules of competition—not just get out of the box, but to build your own box, carving out a unique, memorable space for yourself in your world—a space that attracts the right people toward you and your mission.

The Uncopyable Personal Branding Best Practices

Make standing out from the crowd your operating philosophy, as well as your strategic objective.

Define and Understand Your Moose

The magic doesn't happen without the Moose! Once you know who the Moose is, you can figure out what the right brand promise is. Not before.

Who is your ideal customer? Is it a company or a person? If a company, what industry is it part of, and how can you learn more about that industry? If a person, what is the most likely description of that person? (Think about things like age, gender, education level, and so on.) What problem or challenge does this person face, *in their language?* Is it a problem or challenge you can make go away? How?

How can you be more specific about that? Get much, much clearer about the problem you solve for your Moose. What are the typical signs that a person or organization has this problem? How is this problem first likely to present itself in the Moose's world? What are the implications of *not* solving this problem? Who have you helped to solve this problem in the past? What could you learn about your Moose by talking in-depth to them?

What kind of "Moose bait" attracts that ideal buyer? Where and with whom does your Moose congregate? What does your Moose like to do for fun? How could you make that more fun? What related problems does your Moose typically face—problems that connect to the ones you specialize in disappearing? How could you help your Moose address those related problems in a way that would help you to connect and create an ongoing relationship? What does your Moose want most? How could you get them closer to getting that?

Define Your Brand Promise

Once you know what the right brand promise is, you can start making it and keeping it. Not before!

What value do you enjoy delivering—and get paid for delivering? When have you delivered this value in the past? To whom? Are people willing to pay for it? How do you know?

How is that value experienced by the end user? What, specifically, does it do for them? What positive emotion does the value you deliver make possible? What negative consequences does the value you deliver keep them from having to deal with?

Bearing those answers in mind, what big, specific promise do you make to your ideal customers—your Moose? What concise commitment can you make to your Moose that connects directly to value that you enjoy delivering *and* get paid for delivering? What do your current customers think of this special commitment when you share it with them? How can you make it more concise? More relevant to your Moose's world?

What is the evidence that this promise resonates with your ideal buyer and also makes business sense for you? Who is your best customer? What did they get as a result of working with you? Are they willing to let you create a case study about that? What *narratives* demonstrate to the outside world, in a compelling way, that you keep your brand promise?

Benchmark Outside Your Chosen Industry

Anyone can imitate their direct competitors. Successful personal branding means identifying great ideas from worlds that your competitors haven't even thought of exploring.

What are some best practices from other disciplines, organizations, and fields of activity that are likely to help you connect with and deliver value to your Moose? What great ideas can you adapt from sources that have little or nothing to do with the area in which you compete? Where do you have life experience that your main competitors lack? How can you leverage that experience?

What is a specific example of genius you can steal from another industry? Once you've found this example, how can you test it? With whom? How will you measure whether it supports your brand promise?

How can you use "stealing genius" to stand out from the competition? How can you implement this genius in a way that puts you in a whole different universe from your competitors? What is the best roll-out strategy? How will you confirm that this initiative is perceived as a net plus for your Moose, as opposed to a net negative?

Be True to Your Personal Value Set, Your Mission, and Your Personal and Organizational Rules

What do you stand for? If you don't know, your target market won't know, either. What are you committed to doing, delivering, and denting the universe with? What do you value, personally and professionally? What, in short, is your mission?

What are your rules? What are the operating principles that drive your business relationships with customers? With partners? With the world at large?

What are your values? What do you and your brand stand for? Why? What vision do your values support?

What true story (or stories) authentically defines who you are and what your brand promise is? What is a true *and verifiable* narrative that demonstrates, not just the value you deliver, but the values you *live* by—the kind of person you are?

Create Anchors and Triggers that Uniquely Evoke Your Personal Brand and Promise

Tap into the enduring power of creating anchors and triggers that uniquely evoke your personal brand.

What are your personal brand's unique anchors? (You can have more than one. We have many!) What color or color combination expresses your brand to the outside world? What phrase or phrases?

What images? What triggers in the customer's world will connect to these anchors?

What corner of the Internet do you own, as evidenced by you coming up first when people type in your unique descriptors to a search engine? (For instance: "Uncopyable" and "Muffler Mama.") How much time have you spent developing these descriptors? What do your best customers have to say about them? How do you know for certain that they set you into a whole different universe from your competition?

What triggers real-world conversations with your customers and prospective customers? What issue or problem do they most want to discuss with you? How do they typically express that issue or problem? Should that issue or problem, or its solution, be built into one or more of your anchors?

How can you build or expand your community? How can you reinforce and sustain interactions with customers and others who respond positively to your messaging? Who use your terminology to describe their experiences? Who reach out to you after hearing about your brand and its promise?

Find and Leverage the Right Broadcasting Platforms for Your Personal Branding Message

Master the art of getting your voice, and your message, heard. Connecting with people through the medium of their choice is what keeps your personal brand alive.

Where and when do your Moose congregate today? What new platforms and venues are they using? How can you learn more about those platforms and venues? What can you learn from your best customers about where Moose are hanging out *right now?* (Their migration patterns may have changed since you last checked.)

What attracts them? Once you have identified a spot where your Moose are definitely congregating, ask yourself, *What Moose bait got them here?* How could you offer similar or better Moose bait on this platform?

What keeps them coming back? Once you have identified a spot where your Moose are definitely congregating, ask yourself, *What Moose bait brings them back for more?* How could you offer similar or better Moose bait on this platform?

Know and Play to Your Unique Strengths

Learn to identify value, potential, and branding inspiration in literally every obstacle you encounter. As you master the non-negotiable deliverable of getting your message across to your target audience, you can leverage your life lessons in a way that resonates with that audience.

Identify and focus with total commitment on your own uncopyable strengths. Invest the time necessary to figure out exactly what they are—and aren't. Then plan accordingly.

Where, when, and how do you add value? What is your personal superpower? When was the last time you used it *and* got paid for using it? How could you make that superpower even more awesome? What other superpowers do you have? How do you know?

What are your weak suits? What three things do you *most* wish you could avoid doing during the course of the working day? Could anyone else do these things?

What activities that connect to your weak suits can you delegate? Is there any "weak suit" activity to which you're currently investing time and energy solely out of force of habit? How could you offload these activities? Are any of them activities *no one* needs to do?

Seize Opportunities to Grow from Apparent Setbacks

What are the biggest challenges you've faced and overcome? What are the three biggest challenges that shaped you as a person? What was it about each challenge that motivated you to move beyond your comfort zone? How old were you when you faced each challenge?

How did you respond to them? How, specifically, did you overcome each challenge? What new relationships and resources did you discover and/or nurture? What new ideas did you come up with? What actions did you take?

What did you learn about yourself? How did your vision of yourself change as a result of meeting each challenge? What did you learn about your capacity to adapt and learn? About possibility?

Do any of these have a place in a brand narrative? Of the three challenges you've been examining, which is most likely to resonate with your target audience?

How much time will you schedule to feel bad, angry, or upset about a setback when it happens—before moving on? How much

REMEMBER: PERSONAL BRANDING IS DIFFERENTIATING YOURSELF AND MAKING YOURSELF IMPOSSIBLE TO FORGET—FOREVER.

precious time will you allow yourself to spend on emotions like these? What else could you be doing with that time?

Now go be UNCOPYABLE YOU!

Be sure to get your free resources at
Uncopyableyou.com/resources

ABOUT THE AUTHORS

Steve Miller has been called by *Meetings & Conventions* magazine the "Idea Man" for his non-traditional approach to strategic marketing, branding, and innovation.

Steve calls himself Kelly's Dad and his business title is Marketing Gunslinger. In the increasingly competitive business world today, he teaches organizations how to separate themselves from the crowd. His book, *Uncopyable: How to Create An Unfair Advantage Over Your Competition*, reached #1 bestseller on Amazon.

Since founding The Adventure LLC in 1984, Steve's consulting clients have ranged from solo entrepreneurs to Fortune 100 mega-corporations, including Proctor & Gamble (advising on the Swiffer WetJet product launch), Boeing Commercial Airplane (the 777 launch), Nordstrom, Starbucks, Caterpillar, Philips Electronics, Coca-Cola, and Halliburton, to name a few.

Steve has presented over 1,600 speeches and workshops worldwide for corporations and trade associations in 136 different industries, including the prestigious main TED Conference. (If you're curious about where his TedTalk is, drop him an email!)

In addition to his eight books, Steve has written for and been featured in more than 250 publications, including the *Motley Fool Money* podcast, *Fast Company, Business Week, Fortune, The Wall Street Journal,* and *The Washington Post.*

Follow Steve: linkedin.com/in/steveamiller

Kay Miller is the author of *Uncopyable Sales Secrets: How to Create an Unfair Advantage and Outsell Your Competition.* She was the first woman Amerock ever hired for outside sales. After succeeding in growing her territory with Amerock, she was hired away by Walker Exhaust, the world's largest manufacturer of automotive aftermarket exhaust products. She became the #1 salesperson and earned the nickname "Muffler Mama." Kay's been a top sales achiever ever since.

For many years, she partnered with her husband, Steve, marketing and selling his speeches, consulting services, books, and products. These days, she's an author, speaker, podcaster and consultant. Her passion is helping business owners and salespeople supercharge their sales results.

Kay's favorite title is Kelly's Mom, and she loves spending time with family. She enjoys the outdoors and is an avid skier and hiker. She loves food, wine, animals, and music.

Follow Kay: linkedin.com/in/millerkay

Listen to her podcast, Uncopyable Women in Sales:
uncopyablewomeninsales.buzzsprout.com

Contact Us
UncopyableYou.com
253-874-9665

CONNECT WITH STEVE

 linkedin.com/in/steveamiller

 stevem@beuncopyable.com

CONNECT WITH KAY

 linkedin.com/in/millerkay/

 kay@uncopyablesales.com

Build an UNCOPYABLE life and business

WITH THESE TITLES FROM SOUND WISDOM.

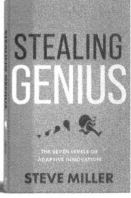

LEARN MORE AT
beuncopyable.com

THANK YOU FOR READING THIS BOOK!

If you found any of the information helpful, please take a few minutes and leave a review on the bookselling platform of your choice.

BONUS GIFT!

Don't forget to sign up to try our newsletter and grab your free personal development ebook here:

soundwisdom.com/classics

PRAISE FOR
UNCOPYABLE YOU

Dive into the transformative wisdom of *Uncopyable You* by Kay and Steve Miller. Discover your unique qualities, create a battle plan, and leverage these insights to enhance yourself and your impact. This book is your guide to unlocking the power of your authentic, uncopyable self.

Mark Hess
Hess Industries Ltd

Steve and Kay Miller's latest book, *Uncopyable You*, offers an insightful and compelling perspective on the importance of personal branding. We're living in an era when everyone is vying for attention, both personally and professionally. Their quote, "Personal branding is differentiating yourself and making yourself impossible to forget—forever," encapsulates the essence of their message beautifully.

Kate Strachnyi
Founder of DATAcated

Uncopyable You is more than a book for me; it was wake-up call to level up my personal branding. For anyone feeling a bit lost in the whole personal branding maze, this book is your personal GPS. It goes beyond just making you look good—it's about digging deep, finding what's genuinely you, and owning it.

Jasmin Bonkowski
Master Your Mindset, Transform Your Life:
Hypnosis for Lasting Success & Balance

In *Uncopyable You,* Kay and Steve offer a clear plan of action and pose the right questions to help identify your niche in any industry. I wholeheartedly recommend this book as an invaluable guide to personal and professional success. It not only inspires but equips readers with the tools necessary to carve out their own path to success. *Uncopyable You* is a must-read for anyone aspiring to stand out in their field and shape a bright future.

Rick Brassfield
Owner, The Hair Lounge

Uncopyable You contains a secret compass to point you toward *your* success. It will help you release strengths within that make you and your personal brand compelling, needed, and *uncopyable.* Brands should be like fingerprints—not copies. Each brand should be unique. It's time to bring out what you've already felt about yourself. Read it and use it so you can share your *Uncopyable You* with the rest of us.

Joe Snyder
Freightliner Custom Chassis
Marketing & Training Manager

Kay and Steve Miller have created a blueprint for engaging our stakeholders in meaningful and memorable ways.

Mark T. Miles, Ph.D.
President & CEO
Orscheln Management Co.

Uncopyable You by Steve and Kay Miller is a must-read for anyone looking to build a standout personal brand, especially in today's AI-driven world. They offer practical strategies for using AI as a tool to enhance, not replace, human connection and authenticity.

Shama Hyder
CEO & Founder, Zen Media

UNCOPYABLE YOU

sound wisdom.
Because Your Success Matters

Sound Wisdom Books by
Steve and Kay Miller

Uncopyable Sales Secrets: How to Create an
Unfair Advantage and Outsell Your Competition

Stealing Genius: The Seven Levels
of Adaptive Innovation

Uncopyable: How to Create an Unfair
Advantage Over Your Competition

UNCOPYABLE
YOU

CREATE A
PERSONAL BRAND
THAT GETS PEOPLE TO
KNOW YOU, LIKE YOU,
TRUST YOU, AND
REMEMBER YOU!

STEVE & KAY MILLER

© Copyright 2024– Steve and Kay Miller

All rights reserved. This book is protected by the copyright laws of the United States of America. No part of this publication may be reproduced, stored in or introduced into a retrieval system, or transmitted, in any form or by any means (electronic, mechanical, photocopying, recording or otherwise), without the prior written permission of the publisher. For permissions requests, contact the publisher, addressed "Attention: Permissions Coordinator," at the address below.

Published and distributed by:

SOUND WISDOM
P.O. Box 310
Shippensburg, PA 17257-0310
717-530-2122

info@soundwisdom.com

www.soundwisdom.com

While efforts have been made to verify information contained in this publication, neither the author nor the publisher assumes any responsibility for errors, inaccuracies, or omissions. While this publication is chock-full of useful, practical information; it is not intended to be legal or accounting advice. All readers are advised to seek competent lawyers and accountants to follow laws and regulations that may apply to specific situations. The reader of this publication assumes responsibility for the use of the information. The author and publisher assume no responsibility or liability whatsoever on the behalf of the reader of this publication.

The scanning, uploading and distribution of this publication via the Internet or via any other means without the permission of the publisher is illegal and punishable by law. Please purchase only authorized editions and do not participate in or encourage piracy of copyrightable materials.

ISBN 13 TP: 978-1-64095-525-7

ISBN 13 eBook: 978-1-64095-526-4

For Worldwide Distribution, Printed in the U.S.A.

1 2024

From Kay

To Steve, my best friend, my partner in business and life. You're still the one!

To Kelly, my daughter, the light of my life, and my inspiration. I'll love you forever.

To YOU, the reader who is committed to being Uncopyable. You've got this!

From Steve

As always, to my girls!

CONTENTS

FOREWORD

"If I had a longer time, I would have
written you a shorter letter."

—Mark Twain

Brevity is the soul of wit, and in this book, Steve and Kay have, indeed, given the reader a "shorter letter" full of wit. In *Uncopyable You*, they have cracked the code and given each entrepreneur, and would-be entrepreneur, a lexicon to one of the most vexing and important facets of organizational development—the personal brand.

Entrepreneurship has been called many things, perhaps the definition I like the most is that state of "relentless pursuit of opportunity with means currently beyond your control." (Attributed to Prof. Howard Stevenson, Harvard Business School, emeritus.) But what the authors, here, are saying is that it is NOT your relentless pursuit, not your *entrepreneur-ness*, not even your amazing product or innovative service that makes you memorable and magical, it is your personal brand. That alone makes an *Uncopyable You*, and to be one of the greats, you cannot go without it.

From the moment I first met Steve, he had my best interest at heart. You know this type of person the moment you meet them. They connect. For years, I have wondered what it was that gave him that 3rd eye, that 3rd ear, the ability to listen and to see and to connect. Now, after reading his latest book, I know. Steve has a radar for authenticity and how to pull it out of your soul. He saw my potential for a personal brand, and he began to pull it out of me. He is persistent and patient, and unrelenting in his belief in this idea. In *Uncopyable You*, he shares his wisdom and gives each reader a window into his method.

Henry David Thoreau is quoted as saying *"Most men lead quiet lives of desperation, and go to the grave with the song still in them."* This transcendental philosophy is as cutting as it is true, but there is good news, this doesn't have to be you. Steve and Kay start at the beginning and build a road map for all types for how to recognize a personal brand and what thought experiments and efforts need to be made confidently to build your own.

Follow this at your own peril (it will change you) ... or don't ... at your own peril you will slink through your effort with a song inside. Steve does not promise it will be easy. It is, of course, work; but it will make you memorable, and in the end, even if the memory of you is one of being shy, quiet and retiring, his pledge is to dig out your very self and to emblazon it on people's memory.

Join the movement of 1—your authentic self—and let Steve and Kay be your guide to this expansion and growth.

John B. Rogers, Jr.
Co-Founder and CEO Haddy Life
"alive in all rooms"